DRUMMER
IN THE WOODS

On quail? No. The grouse had come out to feed on clover leaves. A rare occurrence.

DRUMMER
IN THE WOODS

by

BURTON L. SPILLER

STACKPOLE BOOKS

EDITED BY EUGENE V. CONNETT

———

The First Edition was published in 1962.

Published by
STACKPOLE BOOKS
Cameron and Kelker Streets
P.O. Box 1831
Harrisburg, Pa. 17105

Published simultaneously in Don Mills, Ontario, Canada by
Thomas Nelson & Sons, Ltd.

ACKNOWLEDGMENTS
All the chapters in this book were published in *Field & Stream*, except V in *Cosmopolitan*, Chapters VI and XII in *Outdoors*, and Chapter XIII in *Outdoor Life*. Their permission to use these stories is gratefully acknowledged by the Author.

PRINTED IN THE UNITED STATES OF AMERICA

Library of Congress Cataloging in Publication Data

Spiller, Burton L.
    Drummer in the woods.

    Reprint of the 1st ed., 1962, published by Van Nostrand, Princeton, N.J.
    1. Grouse shooting. I. Title.
[SK325.G7S64   1979]   799.2'48'61   79-19424
ISBN 0-8117-0528-5

Table of Contents

List of Illustrations

DRUMMER
IN THE WOODS

CHAPTER 1

His Majesty, The Grouse

A great cool wood. The murmuring pines and the hemlocks interwoven overhead; with here and there an errant ray of sunlight filtering down on the soft brown carpet beneath. An eager faced ten-year-old boy stealing softly along in the subdued light, a 10-gauge shotgun clutched in his sun browned hands, a thumb hooked over the hammer in the approved Buffalo Bill style, and a stubby forefinger encircling the trigger.

Suddenly the boy stopped, while the great silence of the wood closed in around him. Then from some elusive quarter came a softly whistled *Quit-quit-quit*. From behind a mammoth pine not more than forty feet away a giant cock grouse stepped into view, its head bobbing inquisitively. The blue-black ruff on his neck was lifted until it stood straight out, while his tail was spread fanwise. A flickering shaft of sunlight angling down through a tiny opening far overhead enhanced the beauty of its richly mottled plumage.

The hammer of the 10-gauge clicked softly as the barrel was quietly raised. For a moment the muzzle wavered, then steadied —and Vesuvius erupted with an earth shattering roar. The sun was blotted out, while stars shot dizzily and aimlessly through the heavens, but above all, beyond all, a faint sound dominated the chaos: the spasmodic and drum-like hammering of wings on dry pine needles. The boy heard it even as he tried to staunch the flow of blood from his battered nose. Heard it and staggered forward until he reached the base of the giant pine.

It has been written that Napoleon's chest protruded a trifle more than nature intended, that the laurel wreath upon the brow of Julius Caesar fitted rather snugly at times, and that Alexander the Great had an inflated opinion of his own importance. Ah, me! If only those historians could have seen that boy as he looked down on his first ruffed grouse.

Many, many times since I have stood as I stood then, but there has never been another grouse—or another thrill like that one. The kick is still there, as I presume it still is in the old 10-gauge, but—well—we are a little harder around the heart and shoulders than we were then.

It was inevitable that I should become a grouse hunter, for I had been steeped in grouse atmosphere from the cradle. Father had hunted them until business irrevocably chained him, and even then he would mysteriously disappear for a week or two during the reign of the hunter's moon. Then in the long winter evenings he would tell me stories of his hunting experiences, and always they were stories concerning ruffed grouse.

Thus, in my opinion, grouse became an all important factor. Other boys of my acquaintance might content themselves with slaying elephants and lions and other inconsequential members of the animal kingdom, but I wanted none of that in mine. Nothing but the lordly pa'tridge would satisfy me.

But the open spaces called Dad with a power he could not resist, and we moved to the country. The farm bordered on tide land—hundreds and hundreds of acres of salt marsh, and every pothole on every acre was alive with ducks. Hence the 10-gauge. Even now I cannot look at a gun of that bore without experiencing a slight shudder. We had many a battle together, Old Betsy and I. She loosened many a tooth for me, my nose developed a pronounced twist to port but I mastered her finally. Yes, I could pop both eyes wide open, elevate my eyebrows, pull the trigger, take everything she could hand me and never wink.

With that weapon wing shooting was, of course, impossible, so when I became a man of a dozen years Dad took pity on me and traded the monstrosity for a light, double 12-gauge. Shortly thereafter Hercules and DuPont powder companies began paying dividends on their common stock. I shall always take to myself a modicum of credit for putting them in the black. I burned enough powder that first year to cause that gun to possess approximately the same rigidity as a string of sausage. When Dad inadvertently discovered its condition he condemned it, gave me orders never to shoot it again. Then, making sure he would not be disobeyed, he sold it to a junkman for a dollar and sixty cents.

Thrown thus so suddenly upon my own resources I discovered that although my bicycle was nearly new I had no crying need for it. Also, because I left the house at dawn and returned in the keening dark, a watch was about the most useless bit of portable property I could own. A local merchant, out of the goodness of his heart, took the watch and bicycle, together with the verbal promise to pay the sum of three dollars, in exchange for a second-hand 16-gauge hammerless. It is superfluous to add that hostilities were at once resumed.

With the acquisition of the sixteen I began to kill grouse regularly on the wing. I used the word "regularly" advisedly, for the regularity was truly astounding. I shot at a bird and killed it. Then I shot at forty nine more and missed ingloriously. Then I killed another. And so it went on. *Ad infinitum*. World without end. Amen!

One could do it in those days, for the grouse population seemed limitless. One could walk down an alder run until a bird flushed, then shove the safety ahead, half mount the gun to the shoulder, advance a few cautious steps and another one would go up. About the time one had decided that this was also a miss another one would rocket out. Once again the gun would go BOOM and, as bulging eyes watched the bird's safe departure, experienced fingers would extract the spent shells and slip fresh ones in their places. Then a few steps ahead, grim visaged and determined, and the little drama would be enacted again with all the monotonous sameness of a Punch and Judy show.

It is an irrevocable law that all things must change, and because my shooting could grow no worse it necessarily had to improve. By the time I was sixteen I was bringing home a bird or two each time I went afield. Then, oh wonder of wonders, I broke into fast company.

It happened in this manner. There were three men in our town who had never found the urge to mingle with the higher echelons of our society to be an irresistible one. They worked occasionally in the winter months, and less frequently in summer when the trout were biting. But when the leaves of the maples took on their first autumn tints of red and gold, not even an adverse decision from the United States Supreme Court would have kept them out of the woods. They were grouse hunters, the last unkempt remnants of those scattergun artists who plied their trade in the nineteenth century.

When one of the trio suddenly and much against his wishes was given a one way ticket to his final hunting grounds I received a visit from the two survivors. It seemed that their system of hunting required three men. Would I fill the shoes of the late lamented that fall?

The fool of the world could not have propounded a question to equal that one. I had finished high school that spring, and now my time was my own. Would I fill his shoes? Probably not, but I'd try darned hard.

Thus the ungodly triumvirate was formed, and it proceeded at once to justify its existence. We hunted in fan formation, one man working the runs with a dog, while the other two kept well up on the sides and a little ahead. I can close my eyes now and once more see a bird beating up through the alders, and hear Bill's voice, urgent but somehow calming, calling "Here she comes, kid. Swing a little ahead of her now and take your ti-i-me."

Somehow I killed birds. It is true that I missed many but they still let me shoot on the outside. That fan formation was a great system where the covers were of the character of those we used to hunt. Long alder runs, with oftentimes a tiny brook trickling down through them, and a high bank on either side overlooking the tops of the bushes. Up the center came a man, with a busy dog working close. Twenty yards ahead on either bank the other two kept watchful guard. The majority of the flushed birds went straight ahead, and when they rose above the alders they might as well have been in an open field. Most of the rest broke back over Bill's head—and that was where Bill liked 'em.

I would fail to do justice to the memory of a good man and a good friend if I did not pay tribute to Herb. He claimed he could smell pa'tridge. I think he did have some sixth sense which told him when there was a bird close by. Many a time I have seen him slip his gun from under his arm, turn abruptly and take a few steps either to right or left, and almost invariably put up a bird. Perhaps something within him told him that a bird was there, or perhaps, from his long experience, his judgment told him that this was a logical place for a grouse to be. I do not know the answer. I only know that it was so. Good old Herb! A true friend, and the finest wing shot I have ever known.

We hunted together for two seasons and then I voluntarily severed my connection with them. I had been in a law office since the previous fall. The young attorney there, for some obscure reason, had taken a liking to me, as we say in Maine, and I owe him a debt which I can never repay. In addition to teaching me a few fundamentals of law he opened up for me the rudiments of literature, and delicately, by example, showed me the difference between a sportsman and that reprehensible thing I was fast becoming. He was the first man I had seen who could look down on a beaten salmon and say, "Well, old fellow, you put up a fine fight. You gave me everything you had." Then, as he released the hook: "*Au revoir*. Perhaps we'll meet again next year."

Gradually his influence had its effect. I bought a registered bird dog and became a sportsman.

Then the grouse vanished. Oh, there were some, of course, but they could be counted by tens rather than hundreds. My idolized attorney owned an automobile, if you please, with two horizontal cylinders, a gargantuan horn, and of a color which would make a fireman's shirt turn green with envy. We took a vacation and scoured the state and then through the adjoining one with the same result. So far as worthwhile hunting was concerned, grouse were practically nonexistent. Disconsolately I hunted up Bill. He had rust ropes in the old 12-bore and was dredging clams for a living.

"Don't worry, kid," he advised. "This ain't the first time I've seen 'em go. They'll come back. Maybe next year, or maybe not for two or three years, but they'll come back."

"Didn't we clean up the covers too closely last fall?"

"You know dang well we didn't. I'll bet we left a thousand birds alive right in this one town. Somethin' happens to 'em every once in a while. I don't know what it is, but I do know that they'll come back."

Of course I had to burn powder, so I began hunting the marshes. There were plenty of teal, plump little fellows that came down the wind like bullets. There were black ducks too, and now and then a gaudy old mallard, and while they were not grouse they served their purpose for a time. The next year the grouse were back again. Not in their usual numbers but plentiful enough for good shooting.

Several times since then I have seen grouse diminish in number almost to the vanishing point, but they have always returned. I believe they always will. One thing I am confident of, and that is that hunting can never exterminate them. In late years when there was a scarcity of birds I have taken the trouble to visit covers so remote and inaccessible that I am convinced I was the only person to hunt them that year, and I invariably found that the same scarcity prevailed there. As Bill used to say: "When pa'tridge ain't in one place they ain't anywhere."

I believe that it is always a combination of circumstances which causes the periodic decline. Disease is undoubtedly a factor, as are preditors and poor hatching seasons. When these and a half dozen other factors occur simultaneously it is inevitable that there should be a scarcity of birds. Nature is inexorable. Only the fittest may survive: a tragic rule indeed, but a just one, for only thus may the vigor and stamina of a species be maintained.

I have noticed, too, that when rabbits are plentiful there is usually a fair supply of grouse. The cottontails are easier prey for the meat eaters, and when they exist in quantities the more wily grouse are spared. I have assisted in liberating many snowshoe hares for state officials, for gun clubs and for private individuals and the results have always been the same. Better sport for the rabbit hunters, and many more grouse for me.

To the best of my knowledge and belief there has never been a first class grouse cover in New England without a good background of evergreen trees, preferably pine. The existence of the birds in winter depends in great measure on the size and density of the forest. This winter when the snow is the deepest, go to a stand of dense evergreen, and there where the interwoven branches have prevented the snow from reaching the ground, you will find grouse if there are any in that locality.

A good dog, and he must be a good one, is absolutely essential to the utmost enjoyment of grouse hunting. I do not mean that it is necessary to have a dog in order to kill grouse. There are other systems whereby they may be killed just as dead and in just as great numbers; but I repeat that a good dog is essential to the *utmost enjoyment* of the game.

Setters were my first love and pointers are my present *amours,*

but my observation leads me to believe there is no marked difference between the good ones of either breed. Under present
hunting conditions I would train my young dog to follow a trail
until the bird was found and flushed. Just so long as he was
following scent I would stay with him and give him my moral
support, and we would find that bird if it took the rest of the day
to do it. I would teach him by example that finding birds was
his job and that I would stay with him from soup to nuts.

I do not care to hunt with the man who charts his exact course
before he enters the woods and works his dog accordingly. I
would like to take a straight course and an easy trail myself,
but I am willing to take my birds wherever the dog finds them.
Many and many a time I have seen a dog called off a warm scent
because it chanced to be too far to the right or left of that pre-
conceived straight line. Many a time I have had a dog look me
in the eye and say "There he is again, yelling his fool head off for
me to come in, and I know there's a bird over there. Now what
shall I do?" I have to answer "Better mind him, old fellow. It's
too bad, but you will probably get a trimming if you don't go.
We know the bird is there, and perhaps the next time we come
here he will be on our line of march. Better go back."

I will not whip my dog. I may slap him with a folded news-
paper or my hat, but the whip is out. A whip in the hands of
any man makes him an inferior being. To a certain extent I
believe in the force system of training, but that phrase is far
too often wrongly interpreted. Too many men believe it means
a clubbing each time the dog does a thing to which they, with
their undoubtedly superior knowledge, disagree.

My dog must think more of me than of anything else in the
world. If he does not watch my every move, and follow me from
room to room around the house, he is not worth his salt. The
next requirement must be intelligence, a commodity which he
either has or has not at birth. If he is a moron in the puppy stage
he will always be one. Thirdly, he must have a good nose.

Give me these three qualities in a dog and I will make a shooting companion of him that money cannot buy. If he loves me he will try to do as I wish. If he has intelligence he will develop bird sense and stanchness with but little help from me. If he has a good nose he will find birds. These three things are all that are really necessary.

The frills of dropping to shot and wing are pretty accomplishments but very little else. No good dog will break shot to retrieve when his nose tells him that another bird is lying within dangerously close distance. He will make an occasional mistake but if, as a general rule, he does not know better than to flush birds it is better to find a good home for him and try again. Life is too short to waste any portion of it on a hopeless case.

I said that setters were my first love, and they were, but I remember one pointer who came into my life during that period and won my admiration and respect. He was of royal blood, and as beautiful a specimen as I have ever seen. I met him and his owner when the dog was five years old. Inquiry brought to light the fact that he had not been hunted since he became a year old. He was too fast, too ambitious for his owner, (a young man who had been led to believe that all there was to grouse hunting was the purchase of a dog, a gun and plenty of ammunition, and dragging home the long string of grouse each night.) Disillusioned after a few days afield, he had given it up and made a friend and companion of the dog.

It required considerable urging to get him into the woods again with the dog but he finally consented. The dog had brains and he had a nose. Oh, what a nose! Age had steadied him but he was still very fast, and worked his ground as only a fast dog can do. But he kept within sight most of the time. We found grouse that afternoon. And such points! The memory rises up now within me and I see him again in fancy. A thing of marble, yet radiating all the life and energy in the world. The majestic and immovable hills, a volcano, a tornado, the lightning and the storm all rolled into one beneath that satin skin. It was inspiring. It was almost divine.

I shot over him some for the next five years while his owner grew to love and understand the game. When the dog was ten he became crippled and a pair of youngsters supplanted him; but each fall for four more years a solemn rite took place. I saw it but once, yet it lingers in my memory.

A point to remember.

When the woodcock flight was on, the owner would tenderly lift the old dog into the flivver and drive carefully to one of the better covers. Then he would lift him out, snap the gun together and motion the old dog on. Off he would start, head held high and tail merry, but his poor old legs shaking pitifully. He remembered the cover, though, and knew that this was the best corner. A moment of scenting the wind and he would make an oblique cast, a little spurt of speed, an abrupt slowing up, a few careful steps ahead, and then the old-time point with all the fire and enthusiasm of his youth.

In the interval of silence there would come the shuffling of footsteps as the owner moved in front of the dog, the sudden flutter of startled wings, the upthrust muzzle of the dog as he watched the ascent of the feathered catapault, the crash of nitro, a puff of feathers floating in the air, a retrieved and pocketed bird, a friendly pat on the head—and the solemn rites were over for that year. Perhaps forever.

There were tears in my eyes when I witnessed it. There are tears in them now when I recall the incident. I held no place in his life. I was merely one of the pawns of the game but he won my admiration and respect. If he is roaming the Elysian fields my fondest wish for him is that every alder run contains its quota of woodcock, and each sun-flecked sidehill its covey of grouse.

No man can rightly say that a pointer is better than a setter, or that setters will find more birds than pointers. A good dog is good, no matter what his breed. My personal preference is for a fast dog. The faster the better, so long as he keeps within hearing distance, and I have always used a bell on my dogs. If a dog is good he will slow up when he strikes scent, and the faster he travels before that, the sooner will he find birds.

At the present time in New England a dog must do a certain amount of trailing. More and more frequently I find grouse which run before the dog much in the manner of pheasants. Although we would all prefer to have them lie like woodcock, yet the trait of running can often be turned to the hunter's advantage if he knows the country in which he is hunting.

Unless rushed, a grouse almost invariably tries to put some obstruction between himself and his enemy before taking wing, an inherited instinct gained through eluding the sky raiding accipiters for untold centuries. Also, it prefers a fairly open space for its take-off.

Thus the experienced hunter knows that, if followed carefully through the thick cover, the bird will seldom flush until it reaches the thinner fringe beyond. The method then is to follow behind the dog until, by his point, you know that the bird lies between you and the open space. It is probably crouching in the last bit of cover which fringes the clearing.

The situation calls for two men, who should circle wide and then cut in toward the point where the bird is presumably lying. When once the march is started, do not hesitate. Walk steadily, make no sudden noises and, above all, do not stop. Nothing will startle a bird into flight so quickly as a sudden silence on the part of the hunter. I do not know anything about the reasoning power of ruffed grouse. I do not even know that they possess such a commodity, but I do know that a steady approach will often carry one within a few yards of a bird that a hesitating one would cause to flush well out of range.

Apparently the grouse possesses a one track mind. In the above case the bird undoubtedly says to itself; "Well, I've run as far as I care to. Here's a good place to hop off. If they come much closer I'll just slide across this clearing. I guess they've given it up, though, for they are going the other way now. They're swinging ahead now but they'll pass me a long way off. Oh, oh! They are swinging this way! Coming nearer all the time! If they come much closer I'm going. Yes, I'm going, and I'm going right now. Straight across the clearing to the shelter of the big swamp." And the wise old fool starts. Seven times out of ten he will commit suicide that way when all he had to do to win salvation was to turn and run back past the dog. Had he known enough to stay on the ground he could have played hide and seek with the hunters until they were all gray headed and no harm would have come to him. But no. He had decided to go across the clearing, and he would have tried it if twenty men had stood there with loaded guns.

And that gives rise to a thought to pass along to those sticklers for routine, who turn their dogs with a whistle each time they cast thirty-seven feet and nine inches to the right or left. The next time you hunt that favorite cover of yours, don't go in through Bill Smith's bars as you usually do. Instead, go up to Sam Jones' place and work it backward for a change. Let the dog use his own judgment. He knows more about grouse than you can ever hope to learn.

Go down through the cover that way and see what a demoralized bunch of birds you find. Why, by your one simple act you have upset every plan they have been weeks in perfecting. They never suspected that there was more than one way to hunt that cover. Try it and see if you don't have some interesting experiences.

I shoot a twenty-gauge double and I like it very well indeed. It compensates in part for the natural slowing up which comes after middle age; but if I were trying to bag all the birds it were possible to get I would shoot a twelve. And, believe me, I would shoot it. Many times I have been asked the question "Does trapshooting help your shooting in the brush?" I invariably reply, "Yes. So does shooting my pistol and .22 rifle." If one burns enough powder, hitting automatically becomes a habit.

Although no ammunition manufacturer will agree with me, I still like No. 9 shot in the open barrel during the first part of the open season, with a stiff load of $7\frac{1}{2}$ for a reserve in the other one. As my old friend Herb often remarked; "In shootin' at pa'tridge, all the target you've got is two lead pencils crossed, with a walnut on the end of one of 'em." One pencil represented the backbone, the other the wings, while the walnut was a slightly exaggerated head. "You have to break bones to get 'em," said Herb, and he was right. Grouse will die if hit solidly enough in the flesh, but too often the foxes get the meat.

When a stiff load of No. 9 is shot from a cylinder barrel of a 12-bore, no grouse can fly through the pattern at thirty yards and emerge unscathed—and thirty yards is a long shot in the woods. He who shoots at them at a much greater distance is unwise, while he who reaches out for them at fifty yards is in-human. I would far rather come home empty handed than to come in with the limit and the memory of a hard-hit bird that got away.

I know of but one secret in the art of killing grouse. That secret is concentration. The possibility that a bird may flush at any moment must be always foremost in one's mind. Keep the gun free at all times. Push it over and not under all obstructions. Keep away as much as possible from all thickets which will obstruct your view. Always imagine that a bird is just ahead of you and say to yourself, "This is just a checker game. If I move there, which way will he go?"

At the first hammer of wings the sound must be located. Simultaneously the gun must be mounted and swung in the direction of the sound. Speed and more speed is essential. When the bird breaks into view swing on him and swing fast. Then when you are sure you are right, take about a hundredth of a second to make sure you are sure. When I do that I kill birds consistently and cleanly, but it is one of the hardest things in the world to remember.

Fortunately I carry no lead souvenirs embedded in my flesh, but there have been some near misses. I have been showered with mud on two different occasions when the man behind me was testing the trigger pull on his gun. I have seen the alders suddenly denuded of their leaves within three feet of my head, and by the most careful man with whom I ever hunted. It was my fault, however, for I had worked ahead to turn a running bird and had not advised him of the fact. Three or four years later I got even with him. Nothing but a heaven-placed oak prevented my making a first class salt shaker of him. It was his fault that time, a fact which would have been of little help if I had connected.

I recall another incident when three of us had paused on a little, birch-covered knoll to watch a glorious October sun sink behind the hills. The tired dogs were sleeping at our feet. It was the end of the day. The gray mists rose in the valley below, and the hills nearby were a riot of crimson and gold. The purple

This one is worth two in the bush.

mountains in the distance were rimmed with a band of pure amber, clear cut as cameos against the flaming sky.

As we gazed at that ever new miracle of departing day, out of the blue, from apparently nowhere, a woodcock dropped with a soft little flutter into our very midst.

Then a staid and rather elderly doctor went suddenly mad. Only a modern and exceedingly active battlefield could have compared with it. My hearing has never been the same since, and even now when a shot rings out unexpectedly I find myself searching frantically for a rabbit burrow, a hollow tree, or even a friendly and sheltering bush.

When it was over and the smoke had cleared a little we crawled furtively from our hiding places and looked about. Great yawning shell holes were everywhere, trees were cut off or blown up by the roots. The dogs, mud-spattered and disconsolate, peered furtively at us from a distant knoll. The woodcock, it seemed, had clung to the ground until after the fourth shot. Then, wearying perhaps of its tumultuous welcome, it had decided to search out a quieter bivouac for the night. It went as it came—unhurried, unruffled and unafraid—nor heeded the last salvo which greeted its departure.

Not long ago my companion and I stepped into a wood road at the same instant and some thirty yards apart. At the same moment a grouse flushed at my very feet and flew straight down the road. Involuntarily my gun came to my shoulder and covered the bird. I looked over the barrel into my friend's grinning face.

"I'm glad you're you," he called, then turned his back to me and killed the bird cleanly after it had passed over his head. That hundredth part of a second in which to make sure that you are sure pays dividends at times.

Just now a picture came to me, undimmed by the passage of many years. I could see a gray-clad octogenarian, standing with his back toward a gray sand pile which overlooked a marsh where plover and yellowlegs often fed. His trembling old legs were sprung with the weight of his body and the weary years. He had placed the butt of his gun on the sand before him, crossed his gnarled old hands over the muzzle and rested his wishbone heavily upon them. The gun was a double-barreled 10-gauge. I recognized a 10-gauge in those days as far as I could see one, and I was curious. Circling warily around him, my fascinated eyes at last found what they were seeking. I cautiously approached him.

"Did you know your gun was cocked, mister?" I asked in an awed whisper.

"I allus keep it that way, sonny," he said.

I left him standing there, and what his ultimate fate was I have never learned. I passed by the spot a few days later but he was gone. Whether a hammer had slipped and he had been blown bodily from this mundane sphere, or whether a sudden gust of wind had tipped that devilish tripod into the Atlantic ocean is still a matter of conjecture, although I still recall one more thing in connection with it. I was just a kid then, but I remember thinking that I knew better than to do a thing like that.

Just recently an acquaintance took me to task for spending so much time afield. "Did you ever count the cost of your hunting?" he asked. "Of the time you have lost and the money you have spent?"

I replied, and truthfully too, that I had never lost a moment's time in hunting: that I counted only that time lost which I spent in working.

My acquaintance is the type who believes every argument is won by the person who shouts the loudest; so after he had become sufficiently out of breath to listen for a moment I told him the truth.

"You," I said, "have tended strictly to business for more than a quarter century. Sick or well, winter and summer, through storm and shine, you have missed hardly a day. You have acquired a lot of money. More money than I can even dream of having. I hope you enjoy it, for you have paid a high price for it. A mighty high price. You think the days and weeks and months I have spent afield were wasted. Well, let me tell you this. If such a thing were possible, I would not trade even the memories of those glorious days for all the money you will ever possess."

He told me the exact hyphenated sort of fool I was, and seemed to be offended because I had uttered a simple truth. And it was the truth.

Can memories be measured by gold? If so, then I am rich indeed. Who can value in gold the worth of the memory of that first grouse, of that first double, or of the day when five grouse got up from a brush pile, one after another while I, armed with a pump gun, missed them all. There are thousands of memory bonds stored in the safe-deposit box of my memory, and each has its coupon of happiness and health attached.

How they come trooping back, those memories, undimmed by the passage of time. Was it yesterday that little *Gyp* went off the high bank when the river was in flood, after a crippled grouse and, all unmindful to our cries to come back, swam out into the full force of the current? Then down through the white water he went, rolling over and over, now lost to view, now emerging for a moment and still fighting valiantly. Was it yesterday that I waded into the backwash at the foot of the rapids and gathered him in my arms, half drowned but with the bird still in his mouth.

No, that was not yesterday, for faithful little *Gyp* has been sleeping on the sunny bank below the old willow these many, many years.

Was it yesterday that Vaughn's pointer went down the river and out over the bar into the storm tossed Atlantic after a broken winged shelldrake? I remember how we watched him from the shore until his head was but a mere speck in the distance, and then that, too, disappeared. Then, because the wind and tide set toward the east, we went a mile upriver to the bridge, crossed it and came back to the beach on the other side, hoping against hope that we might find his body.

I remember how, as we stood gazing out over that welter of wind-driven water, Vaughn's sudden, exultant shout rang out. "By God! There's my dog!" And there he was, fighting his way in through the breakers, with the shelldrake, still alive, in his mouth.

No, that was not yesterday, for I have not seen Vaughn for more than twenty-five years.

Phantom days. How vividly I recall them. Hundreds and hundreds of days and thousands and thousands of scenes over many hundreds of miles. Would I trade these memories for money? Would I? Ha!

But of all those golden days which I can so readily recall, there are two which stand apart in my memory.

The first happened on the day before Thanksgiving. Gene and I had regretfully decided that this should be the last day of the season, for other interests would claim us after the holiday. With a fresh dog we motored to a distant cover where we knew there were plenty of grouse.

Arriving there, we found that both dog and birds were extremely wild. We had a few points, but the birds would not lie, and persisted in getting up well out of range. By lunch time we were so completely demoralized that when at last a pair of birds got up almost at my very feet I missed them both cleanly. Disgusted with ourselves, the dog, the birds and the world in general, we decided to shake the dust of that cover from our feet, nevermore to return—until next year.

We ate our lunch, drove to another cover some five miles distant and sent the dog in. A few minutes later he came to a beautiful point. Two grouse got up simultaneously, breaking nicely for me, and I bagged them both. Shortly after that Gene scored. We went up one side of the cover. The dog gave us seven perfect points, we flushed eight birds and bagged them all with eight shells.

On the long way home we fell to discussing the events of the day. It was just too bad, Gene remarked, that we were forced to wind up the season in such a manner. We should have been permitted to shoot until one of us missed. Before reaching home we decided to start at daylight next morning, go to a nearby cutoff where we knew grouse were feeding, and shoot until one of us missed his bird.

We were off before sunrise, and a half hour later the dog was on point. A grouse got up, and Gene, shooting directly into the sun, brought it down. Working down through a draw, we swung about and came back across a broad flat. The sky was cloudless, and a light, cool, west wind had sprung up which, combined with the warming sun at our backs, set every nerve atingle.

The dog roaded over in front of me, doubled up like a half opened jack-knife and stopped. It was an ideal layout. Nothing but brush and tangled vines underfoot, and not a brush or tree within two hundred yards. I grinned and stepped in front of the dog.

W-h-i-r-r-r!

A bird got up beside me, just clearing the tops of the brush piles, and going like a bullet for the distant cover. I killed her cleanly and ordered the dog to fetch. He went a few feet ahead—and stopped. Slipping in a fresh shell, I stepped before him once more.

W-h-i-r-r-r!

An old cock grouse hammered up into the wind, straight ahead and close, just where I like to have them. I looked over the barrels, and such was the angle of his ascent that I could see each feather on his back, his wings and his wide spreading tail.

I pulled the trigger. A puff of feathers snapped from him and floated down in the breeze. The wings momentarily ceased their beat as he hung suspended in mid air. Then, in that instant when I looked for him to collapse, he righted himself and with a wild flutter of wings banked sharply to the right. Instantly I gave him the other barrel, and again feathers zipped from him as he hung up for a moment, but once more he righted himself, swung a little more to the right—and there was good old Gene with his pump.

Bang!

A puff of feathers.

Bang!

More feathers.

Bang!

Wing feathers, tail feathers, all kinds of feathers came floating down but the grouse went on and on, across the wide flat and into the woods nearly three hundred yards away. Gene scratched his head bewilderedly. "Well, I'll be damned!" he said. "I guess we can go home now."

Under the circumstances, going home seemed to be the proper thing to do; but first we went down to where the grouse had entered the woods. The dog made a short cast and winded game, roaded ahead cautiously, and came to a point near a giant pine. We went in eagerly, prepared to lay down another barrage, but it was unnecessary. The valiant old fellow lay dead at the foot of the pine.

Memories, memories. How they come trooping back. Countless incidents which rise, unbidden within me and make of every day afield a hallowed memory. I have had many hobbies and ridden them hard, but grouse shooting is the only one which still holds all the old fascination. I have looked over a gun barrel at almost every species of New England game. I have fought it out with the lordly salmon on light tackle, and have met the bass that was my master. I have been thrilled, excited and entranced by those experiences, but my heart has never indulged in the

CHAPTER 2

Thunder King

With a spasmodic convulsion of his frail body *Thunder King* burst the last of his prison's restraining wall and collapsed on the litter beneath him. Around him a life giving heat radiated, and in the grateful warmth his wet little body soon dried and the protecting down which clothed him straightened and fluffed about him.

He moved his body slightly, drew his legs beneath him and achieved an upright posture. Dimly he became aware of movement in the darkness about him: of faint little chirps and whisperings, and of the feeble tap-tap-tap of his less hardy brothers and sisters as they pecked intermittently at the still unbroken shells of their prisons.

Of the eleven eggs in the nest, *Thunder King's* had been the first to open, but before the night had vanished the eleventh shell had parted and the eleventh ruffed grouse had hatched. The later arrivals still sprawled where they had collapsed, but in *Thunder King* the throbbing, pulsing life which is the heritage of his kind was already asserting itself.

The warmth giving body above him lifted slightly as the female grouse fluffed her feathers the better to shield her brood. *Thunder King* blinked at the sudden fierce brightness which beat upon his eyes. Straightening on legs which were already sturdy and strong, he pushed his way through the restraining feathers and thrust his head out from under the drooping wing.

An early May sun bathed the hillside about him, and the air was heavy with the scent of arbutus. The nest was built between two protruding roots of a huge sugar maple, and the sun, beating down upon it, heated the tiny niche until warm wisps of vapor danced in the cooler strata of air above it. *Thunder King* pushed boldly out and gazed over the section of New Hampshire which was to be his domain.

Before him the ridge fell away in a gradual descent to a swampy valley. Beyond the swamp it rose once more in a series of rolling foothills, then swept abruptly upward in a rock-scarred formation whose summit was lost in the low hanging clouds. The sun rose higher and swung gradually toward the south. Then the mother grouse moved. Her bent legs straightened and she stood erect. By an almost imperceptible movement she caused her feathers to stand straight out from her body. A chick, buried deeply in the heavier feathers of her breast struggled to retain its position, then dropped lightly among its fellows.

The grouse stretched higher, shook herself lightly, settled her feathers smoothly about her fever wasted frame, stepped daintily from the nest and emitted a faint clucking sound. Instantly every chick stood erect among the litter of broken shells, looked about for a moment, then scrambled up from the crude depression and followed her. For perhaps twenty feet she enticed them with her seductive calls, then fluffed her feathers lightly, extended her wings and gathered her little flock beneath her.

By such easy stages she succeeded, in the course of an hour, in drawing her brood a hundred yards away from the nest. Their progress had been unhurried. At each forward step she pecked among the dead leaves and disclosed many minute particles of food; a weed seed here, an insect there, and new shoots of greenery everywhere. With each find the chicks clustered closely about her and pecked at the microscopic bits of food she disclosed, or tugged with puny strength at a part of some mangled insect which protruded from her bill.

Before the sun had set she led them into a profusion of dead and tangled fern. Here they spent the night, hovering close beneath the enveloping feathers. Not until the morning sun had dried the dew about them did the old bird stir.

More active and a full third larger than any of his fellows, *Thunder King* was yet one of the most delicately fragile bits of bird life capable of foraging for itself. To most of the feathered youngsters of the wild, Nature grants the boon of parents who will bring them food until their full size is attained. But by the time they were forty-eight hours old the brood of young grouse were foraging about and discovering much of their food for themselves. Although they clustered about their mother when she announced the discovery of a choice bit of food, their chief need for her was in the comforting warmth of her body through the hours of the night.

When they first emerged from their shells their wet little bodies were scarcely larger than the first joint of one's middle finger. Now, in only a week, they had doubled in size, while through the soft down of their wings a row of mottled brown feathers was becoming plainly visible. In a few more weeks their bodies would be clothed in a rough but serviceable coating of feathers capable of turning a sudden shower, and of retaining their body heat through the cool nights.

Before that event occurred, however, the skies clouded, a chill wind blew in from the east and rain began to fall. For two nights and a day the old grouse hovered her brood, but hunger drove them forth at last. Fortune favored them almost at once, for their course brought them to an ant hill where a foraging skunk had been digging for the larvae. Now, in the driving rain, the valiant workers were engaged in repairing the ruined galleries, and scurrying hither and yon with their embryo young.

The birds ate their fill, but they were drenched and chilled by the rain, and when the old bird called them forth next morning into a world bathed in sunshine, only seven heard and answered the call.

Of the seven, *Thunder King* was the strongest. His legs were sturdy and straight, and he moved in a series of short rushes which were unbelievably fast. It was this inherited trait which saved his life before he was two weeks old. They were skirting the base of a giant pine when a black shadow separated itself from the equally black shadows around it and dropped, plummet-like, into the midst of the little band. The old grouse was a few feet in advance of her offspring, but she caught a flash of the falling body and emitted a shrill, whistling cry. Then, even as she uttered it, she dashed with outstretched wings at the thing which was menacing her brood.

That warning cry was *Thunder King's* first intimation of danger. Despite the fact that he was hearing it for the first time, his muscles responded instantly. The dropping form was close above him, the black claws thrust down to crush him to earth, but in the moment which was his he moved from under that shadow of death. With the speed and accuracy of a snake the crow struck at him, with wide open beak, as he scurried for safety. The blow missed by inches. Then a brown ball of fury hurtled past him and, with stiffly set wings, beat a ringing tattoo about the head of the enemy. The crow tried once to strike her with his lance-like beak, but the very fury of her attack robbed him of his power to harm. With a raucous cry he turned and fled from the scene.

Not until his retreating form had vanished from sight did the mother relax her vigilant attitude. Then her ruffled feathers sank and she called her brood with a series of faint, whistling chirps. Ere the call was completed, seven inanimate and shapeless leaves stirred, stood erect and moved toward her across the sun flecked earth.

Two weeks of perfect spring weather passed with only one brief shower to endanger the lives of the brood. Then death struck again.

A wandering mink had left the stream he had been following, to make a foray on the higher land. Primarily a fish eater, he was nevertheless not averse to a bit of red meat, so when his nose caught the scent of grouse he followed it. So cunning had been his approach that his spring, when he launched it, was a matter of mere inches. His sinuous body flashed through the air, and a forefoot flattened a victim lifeless to earth.

Thunder King had seen and understood that menace as it struck, and he darted away. Then, even as he ran, his tiny wings took up a vibrating beat, his plump little body lifted and soared aloft. A moment later he looked down on his enemy from the vantage point of a limb some five feet above the ground.

With his rounded ears flattened back against his wicked head, his brilliant eyes glowing with an unholy fire, the mink seized the luckless young grouse in his jaws and glared about. Once again the mother went into action with one of the instinctive stratagems of her kind. Uttering a piteous, wailing cry, she thrust one wing limply down, crouched sidewise in a perfect imitation of a badly crippled bird, and fluttered weakly away.

It is a superb bit of acting which has fooled many a farmer's boy, and the mink was no more sagacious. To spring upon the thing which cried and mewed and fluttered before him seemed easy. His lips curled backward wickedly, while the dead bird dropped, forgotten, from his jaws as he sprang in swift pursuit.

Few of the four footed things of the wild can match the mink's quickness of movement, but in the game of tag she was playing with death the grouse was the master every moment. The leaping body of the mink flashed bewilderingly as he tried his utmost to close upon her, but his best endeavor was never quite enough.

Always beyond him, drawing him with each leap farther from her little brood, she led him on and on, down the bank and along the edge of the swamp, until the mink realized the futility of the chase and stopped.

Again she tried to seduce him, fluttering dangerously close while his eyes glowed red with baffled lust. Then, when she knew her work was done, her body assumed its former grace, her bent pinions straightened, and the hill echoed the thunder of her wings as she zoomed upward over the trees and back to her little flock. The brood responded instantly to her crooning call and, with never a thought of the stricken one, they hurried away through the leafy aisles to safety.

By September the young birds were more than two-thirds grown. The swamp had furnished coolness through the summer days as well as an unfailing food supply. Now they had emerged from it and were feeding on the ripened blackberries in the foothills. With the first frosts they moved higher and came, at last, to an amphitheater in the hills which proved to be a veritable Mecca.

A century ago the land had been cleared and a tiny settlement had come into being, but time had rotted the buildings and leveled the pitifully crude stones in the little cemetery. The forest had reclaimed its own, but man had left a heritage to the woodfolk that roamed the wilds where once had been fertile fields.

Into this mountain domain the settlers had brought a few apple trees. They had flourished and their plump seeds had been scattered far by the squirrels. Now countless young trees had sprung up over the hundreds of acres, and spilled their fruits upon the ground with the coming of fall. It was ideal grouse country, for the apples were nourishing and sweet, and the supply was adequate for the needs of all the lesser forest folks. Into this paradise the little flock of grouse came, and into it, later, came John Thornton.

It was mid-October. The frosts had already seared the birch leaves, tingeing them a delicate russet, while the maples were a riot of crimson and gold. The ripened apples hung precariously by their weakened stems, or dropped heavily to earth with each passing breeze.

Beneath one of these trees *Thunder King* was feeding with a young female of his kind. Whether it was one of his own kin he was not destined to know, for the area sheltered several small flocks and they mingled together promiscuously. They were nearly full grown now: in fact, the young cock had already attained the average size, being a full sixteen inches in length, and weighing twenty ounces. His variegated plumage, brown and black and gray, was of that peculiar slatey cast occasionally seen among certain members of his clan. His long tail was capable of opening into a perfect fan, across the lower circumference of which a broad, black band stretched. His head was adorned with a tiny crest, while at each side of his neck a blue-black ruff stood out from the shorter feathers around it.

Pecking at one of the apples, *Thunder King* suddenly lifted his head and listened. An alien sound had reached him: the sound of feet pattering stealthily among the crisp leaves somewhere behind him. Then, from a greater distance, he heard a twig snap sharply and, a moment later, another.

In his five and one-half months of life *Thunder King* had seen many a wandering deer, and a bear on two different occasions. Almost daily some clumsily shuffling porcupine would cross his path, but he had never been alarmed by their presence or the sound of their footsteps.

Although the noise was not one whit different than those others, something stirred within him and he was suddenly afraid. From out the past the voices of ten thousand ancestors were crying that this new presence was the epitome of danger: that it was the very embodiment of death.

Thunder King turned and uttered his cry of alarm. At its first note his companion crouched and became one with the fallen leaves about her, but the cock moved warily away.

Beyond the open space beneath the tree a clump of gray birches stood, their bases hidden by fern clumps and tangled vines. Through this screen *Thunder King* forced his way until he came to the outermost edge of the protecting cover. There he paused to listen. Behind him all was still save for the stirring of the leaves as a breath of wind fanned them. Once more a twig snapped under a heavy foot. *Thunder King* crouched a little and became suddenly tense.

John Thornton was swinging easily along with the tireless stride of a man who has tramped many a woodland trail. In the crook of his right arm a shotgun rested, while his left hand was free to ward off the branches that whipped about his face. His loose fitting khaki coat was stained and brier frayed, and the game pocket bulged across his hips from the two grouse it held.

Ahead of him a black and white setter worked busily. His perfectly chiseled head was held high as his expanded nostrils quested the air, his plumed tail was stiffly out-thrust as he quartered back and forth across the trail the man would presently tread.

Suddenly the dog stopped. His upthrust muzzle went even higher while his nostrils quivered visibly. A moment he stood thus. Then he went slowly and cautiously ahead. With each step his body became more tense. Every nerve and sinew seemed to tingle with an unseen but dynamic force.

For a matter of twenty feet he advanced thus. Then, even as he was taking another forward step, some power over which he had no control stoped him in the very midst of that movement. His body stiffened, became lifeless, statuesque, an immobile thing of marble or of bronze. Only his nostrils moved, expanding and contracting as they drew in the rich body scent. *Duke,* true to the instinct inherited from his ancestors, was pointing a close lying grouse.

"Steady, boy." Thornton breathed the words quietly as he withdrew the gun from the crook of his arm. "Where is she?" The modulated tones seemed to blend and become a part of the murmuring silence of the woods. "Where is she? Under that apple tree? All right. I'll kick her out." He thrust the gun forward and moved carefully ahead.

Crouched behind the friendly screen of brush, *Thunder King* waited with every nerve tense. A twig snapped again, and instantly the air reverberated with the thunder of beating wings as the female rocketed upward from the place of her conceal-ment. Her hurtling, brown body had almost reached the tops of the birches above him when a crashing report rang out. For a moment the stricken bird seemed to hang suspended in mid-air as a puff of feathers drifted from her body. Then her wings went limp and she collapsed, lifeless, and came plummeting down.

From the time the grouse had started her flight until she was dead in the air above him had been no more than a split second, yet *Thunder King* was already in motion. Instinctively his nimble feet propelled him forward with incredible speed, while his wings took up their tremendous driving beat. Directly in his path a lone sapling loomed menacingly, but even as his speed increased he twisted his wide flaring tail and veered abruptly around it.

That movement saved his life, for in the instant of his turn-ing the gun crashed again, and shot whistled and hissed past him, while a searing flame stabbed his side. He flinched at the sudden sting, and his wings missed a beat. Then he righted himself and soared up over the distant treetops.

"You dog-gone amateur," Thornton reproached himself. "That bird was in the open and you let him get away. Touched him up a bit, though. I saw a feather or two. Well *Duke*, fetch the other and we'll follow this one up. We can't leave a crippled bird to suffer. Fetch, boy."

Had it not been for the pain of his wound, *Thunder King* would have set his wings at the termination of his first soaring rush, and planed for a hundred or more yards in a gradual descent to earth, but the hurt lent added terror to his soul, so that his flight carried him a quarter mile before he ceased his driving wing beat. Ahead, a towering pine thrust its top above the surrounding trees. *Thunder King's* body tilted upward while his outstretched wings gripped the air. His speed checked abruptly as he slid through the pine limbs and perched on a branch near the tree trunk.

For twenty minutes he sat thus, unmoving and silent. Then, as he caught the sound of movement in the distance, his body stiffened and his neck elongated and stretched upward. With that one movement his identity vanished and he became a perfect replica of a broken branch of the pine on which he sat.

The sounds came nearer, then veered and passed to the left. Presently they ceased entirely, but for many long minutes the bird sat as rigidly immovable as an inanimate thing. Then his posture became less tense and he shifted his position slightly. The sting was sharp in his side, and the feathers above the wound were matted and wet. He moved again until his body rested against the tree trunk.

The sun slid lower and hung poised above the distant mountains as lengthening shadows crept up the valley. Later, the stars came out and the night wind moaned in the branches, but *Thunder King* still sat on his perch, the pain still burning in his side, and the blood soaked feathers hardening about the wound.

Now it was spring again. *Thunder King* stood on a fallen log and looked out over the valley. At the base of the mountains the snow still lay in ten-foot drifts, but here around him the ground steamed in the sunshine.

The winter had been a severe one, but the young cock had survived where a less hardy creature would have known a speedy death. His wound had healed quickly, and he was once more physically fit when the deep snows came. The apple trees had proved to be a priceless boon then, for their succulent buds are one of the choicest delicacies known to ruffed grouse.

With others of his kind *Thunder King* fed upon the nutritious buds until his crop was extended to the size of a baseball. Then, with folded wings he had plunged headlong into the snow, where he remained warm and protected while fierce storms raged above him.

Now he stood on the log and looked out over his little world. A sound reached his ears, a sound which was new to him although it was as old as the ageless hills. *Boom-boom-boom!* Deep and vibrant it echoed across the valley. Deep and vibrant as the sound of a muted drum.

Listening to that distant beat, the bird knew a swift transformation. The tiny crest on his head lifted, his purple neck ruff stood straight out while his tail spread in a perfect fan. Rearing upright, he thrust his wings stiffly out before him and away from his swelling breast. Then with a sudden movement he brought them almost together before him, and a great, hollow *BOOM* beat upon the morning air. *BOOM.* The beat was faster now. Faster and faster, until the movement of the wings became an indistinguishable blur, and the sound merged and blended into a continuous roll.

From the first beat until the last diminishing flutter, perhaps ten seconds had elapsed. Now, at its expiration, his body lost all its tenseness. His ruff settled, his fan closed, and he strutted the length of his log and listened. Faint and far across the valley the challenge echoed once more, and after a moment he answered it.

The sun rose higher and the teeming hillsides beckoned, but still *Thunder King* paced his log and sent out his intermittent battle challenge; but save for the echoing drum of his distant rival there was no other sound. Then he caught a glimpse of brown as it moved across a bar of sunlight, and caught the faint murmur of hesitant feet.

Presently a plain little female emerged from a tangle of dried ferns, and paused to look up at the lordly figure above her. *Thunder King* stretched his wings downward until their tips brushed the log, then pirouetted to display his grace. The female hesitated, plucked a wind blown seed from the ground at her feet, then came shyly nearer.

Once more *Thunder King* stood stiffly erect and sent his tri-
umphant challenge echoing across the valley. Then he dropped
down from the log and advanced to meet his bride.

Again it was October, and once more *Thunder King* was
pecking at a fallen apple. From far down the valley a shot
echoed. He ceased his feeding and stood erect in a listening
attitude, whistling as he did so his soft little *Quit-quit-quit* of
alarm.

A quarter hour passed, and then he heard the sound for which
he had been waiting—the pattering feet of a dog, and the heavier
tread of a man coming up the valley as they had come on that
other memorable day. He paused only long enough to definitely
locate the source of the sound, then turned and ran at surprising speed in the opposite direction. Through juniper brush
and tangled fern he sped, then on through a thicket of young
pine and a clump of drooping alders. Not until he had passed
this last bit of cover, did he stop, and then only momentarily.
With a thunderous roar of wings he took off, flying low across
the open. Not until he had flown for thirty yards did he zoom
upward to clear the treetops.

John Thornton, pushing hurriedly along after the trailing
Duke, stopped at the sudden tumult and threw his gun halfway
to his shoulder. Then he lowered it and spoke to the dog.

"Too far, *Duke.* That was an old one with a college education. Boy, he was a real one though. Did you see the size of him
when he cut up into the skyline? Well, we can't always be lucky
—and neither can he. We'll look him up again about day after
tomorrow. He'll be back here by that time. Yes, sir, we're sure
going to get a crack at that fellow before the season is over."

John Thornton had been hunting grouse for more than
twenty years and had learned to know the true definition of the
word "sportsman." It had been years since he had shot a sitting
bird or one which his dog had not pointed. Of late there were

few of the latter, for *Duke* was developing into one of those treasures which are far too uncommon—a genuine grouse dog.

Although the dog missed but few, Thornton was prone to let many an easy kill slip away without a shot. The game held all its old-time fascination, but he had learned that its chief joys were not in coming home each night with the daily limit. Many a bird lived to perpetuate his kind because the man was content to know he could have exacted the death penalty had he cared to press the trigger.

Despite the fact that his killing was often tempered with mercy, he found a keen delight in outwitting a shy old bird, and often he would spend days in the accomplishment of the task, grinning good naturedly at each defeat, but visualizing with keen anticipation the moment when the wary one waited a moment too long before taking wing. When *Thunder King* had outguessed him for the third time, he delivered an ultimatum to the rapidly disappearing form.

"All right, old fellow," he said. "You've been having your fun, but now it's my turn. Next time I'll get here while you're eating breakfast, and I'll camp on your trail until I get one close shot at you if I have to stay a week. Did you understand what I said, *Duke?* He's fooled us long enough. It's up to us to show him that we know something about this game too."

The morning sun was not more than an hour high when *Thunder King* heard them coming. This time the sound came from a different direction, for Thornton knew that many a grouse had made the fatal mistake of flying its customary route even when danger threatened from that quarter. As the bird heard the sound he hesitated only for a moment. Then, as he caught the glint of sun on a gun barrel, he hurtled up into the air until the foliage of the trees hid him, whereupon he planed off in level flight on a line which effectively screened him until he was well away. Thornton chuckled as he came up to the dog.

"That's all right, old boy," he said. "We're learning some-

thing about him. He goes straight away from what he thinks
is the danger point. We'll remember that if things work out
right. Go on. Let's keep right after him."

At the termination of his hundred yard flight the old cock
had dropped earthward in a long, swooping, glide which carried
him an additional hundred yards. He struck the ground lightly,
ran a few steps, then walked through a thicket and stopped to
listen.

It was not long before he again heard the approach of the
man and dog. Once more he took wing, scaling along close to
earth, and dodging in and out among the tree trunks with a
speed and accuracy which no other bird can equal.

"All right, *Duke*," Thornton said again, as he listened to the
thundering takeoff. "We'll keep right after him. This time he
won't go quite so far."

The man was correct. *Thunder King* did not know that his
stubby wings were wholly inadequate to sustain the weight of
his body in extended flight, or that the tremendous exertion of
lifting his body several times in quick succession took fearful
toll from his wing muscles. Before him lay an opening, a portion
of field which the forest had not yet quite reclaimed. It was
scarcely more than a hundred yards in extent, yet the bird knew
a sudden reluctance to cross it. Veering sharply to the left, he
came to rest within a short gunshot of the opening.

Presently he heard them coming. As they were not dangerously close yet he waited. A moment later the sound of the foot-
falls ceased. He remained alert, listening. Once he thought he
heard the low murmur of a voice but he was not sure. All was
quiet now. Not a twig snapped or a leaf stirred. He waited.

"Whoa, boy," Thornton whispered, as *Duke* once more drew
scent. "He's this side of the clearing. You stay right where you
are, and don't you move a step until I whistle."

He shook an admonitory finger at the motionless dog, backed
quietly away and struck off at a right angle to their previous

course. Circling carefully, he came at last to the open field. He
followed the edge of the wood then, walking soundlessly in the
dew drenched grass. Presently he came to the position he coveted. Drawing the gun from beneath his arm, he hitched his
sleeves up at the wrist, emitted a soft whistle, and chuckled in
quiet satisfaction.

Thunder King heard *Duke* as he made his first forward step,
and knew it was time to move. He turned and ran toward the
opening where John Thornton, with gun ready, awaited his
coming. Crouching low, he hurried along under the friendly
brush, pushed through the last bit of cover—and looked up into
the eyes of the waiting man.

"Now," said John Thornton, "just which way do you think
you're going?"

Thunder King made his decision instantly. He whirled like a
flash of light, ran directly back toward the advancing dog, and
not until less than a score of feet separated them did he take
wing. Then he flashed upward with a glorious rush, swung in
behind a low pine and slid safely away.

John Thornton chuckled delightedly as he once more cradled
the gun under his arm. "He fooled me," he said to the dog. "I
thought he would come across the clearing. He's smart, but he'll
wait a second too long before the day is over. Come on, boy. Get
after him."

Again *Thunder King* was terminating his flight. With drooping wings stiffly set he was coasting down for a landing. Suddenly something dropped, on hissing pinions, from the blue
above him. He sensed it instantly, and knew it to be the dreaded
raider of the skies—the deadly goshawk.

Once again his reaction was instantaneous. He veered sharply
downward, banked with what power he could in the fraction of
time allotted him and crashed, head on, into a tangled juniper
bush.

The branches had scarcely closed behind him when the long,

hooked, talons of the hawk struck at the spot above him, but
Thunder King had won his sanctuary with a scant foot to spare.
Through the protecting boughs he saw the hawk glide effortlessly upward to a perch on a weathered limb, then peer down
at the place of his concealment with hard and cruel eyes.

With all thought of his former peril forgotten, the grouse
crouched in his scanty shelter, and knew that his present plight
was the worst he had ever faced. Were the cover extensive
enough he might perhaps steal away an inch at a time without
being detected, but the juniper was hardly six feet in diameter,
and the next bit of cover was twenty feet away. To attempt to
reach it would be madness, and should he resort to flight those
talons would sink into his flesh before he had freed himself
from the branches around him.

There was but one thing to do, and that thing was to crouch
where he was and wait, perhaps for hours, for the killer was
tireless in his waiting, and only darkness could rob him of his
prey. *Thunder King* obeyed the instinct inherited from his ancestors and crouched there immovable and still.

The October sky was cloudless, and not a leaf was stirred by a
vagrant breeze. Then, in the absolute stillness, the grouse
caught a faint tremor of the earth. He listened. After a moment
he heard it again and knew it for what it was: the stealthy tread
of a dog creeping up behind him.

On noiseless feet, his gun outthrust before him for instant
action, John Thornton came up behind the rigidly pointing
Duke, his eyes riveted on the juniper, and an anticipatory little
smile wrinkling the corners of his mouth. As quiet as had been
his approach, *Thunder King* heard it and knew once more all
the oldtime terror. The peril which lurked above him was forgotten. It was man who was there behind him. Man! The killer!

Thunder King came out of the juniper on glorious wings.
From the branch above him the gray hawk stooped unerringly,
even as Thornton's gun leaped to his shoulder. As his finger was

closing on the trigger his eye detected that falling meteor. With an almost imperceptible movement he elevated the muzzle a trifle and pulled the trigger.

Unconsciously he lowered the weapon, broke it, tossed away the shell and slipped a fresh one in its place. Then he went slowly ahead and stood over the fallen bird. The cruel beak still opened and closed spasmodically. The curved talons were sunk deeply in a bit of rotten wood. He stirred the mottled carcass with his toe and felt a deep satisfaction.

"It was you he was afraid of, eh?" he said, as he slid the gun back under his arm. "Well, there'll be no need of his fearing either of us again. Come on, *Duke.*"

CHAPTER 3

Four Mile Grouse

The Four Mile Pasture is a paradise for grouse. It is approximately a mile in width, while its length is indicated by its name. It lies between two mountain ridges which lack but little of achieving a true perpendicular. In theory it is a valley, but in effect it is a plateau, for it is high country in the foothills of New Hampshire, and except for the towering walls which flank its length, would in itself be a mountain-top. It is well hidden and particularly inaccessible and for that reason is not well known, but it is one of the best covers on my personal map.

The walls temper the winter winds, while numerous patches of pines afford added protection. Berries grow profusely in the openings, and sumac, thorn apples and barberries furnish additional food. Scattered here and there throughout its length are thrifty young apple trees. Close in around the entire length of the rocky walls a band of black birches stretches. The buds of these furnish an unfailing winter supply of food, and they are plentiful enough to feed a thousand grouse.

It was here that Gene and I came, after wandering an unbelievable number of miles in Maine and New Hampshire, for the insanity which afflicts grouse hunters is just a bit different from that which other sportsmen enjoy. Despite all evidence to the contrary, he will insist that black is white, or that the sun customarily rises in the west. Even a mediocre salesman could take his order for a slice of green cheese from the moon, and one must needs be a hypnotist to make him believe there is a scarcity of grouse.

"Heck!" he will say. "Look at the number of birds we left

last fall. Look at the hatching season. We never had better weather. There are birds enough if we can only find them."

He believes it, too, with the simple faith of a zealot, and will not admit the possibility of his being wrong. Hope springs eternal in his breast, and he goes on, like Tennyson's brook, forever.

For the first month of the open season we had scoured the nearer covers in both states from morning to night, with a dismaying lack of luck. We found birds, for almost every good cover had a few in it, but nowhere were they plentiful enough so that we could conscientiously take more than an occasional one for the benefit of the young dog I was working.

But when at last we came to the Four Mile Cover we found birds. We had gone through it casually with two dogs, a camera and only one gun, for Gene is a true conservationist and will not take even one bird unless he believes there are enough left for seed. But here at last were enough to satisfy him.

"Twenty seven!" he said, when at last we came out. "And we didn't so much as throw a stone at one of them. Let's give them time to settle down, and then come back and have a real old-time day."

I agreed. When we came back after three days I could see that he meant business. Usually he dons a voluminous and many pocketed coat which he stuffs full of check cords, shells, spike collars, bells, whistles, lunch, his camera and other impedimenta. Now he pulled on a sleeveless jacket, distributed a box of shells evenly in his pockets, so that no accumulated weight might mar the smoothness of his swings, hung his camera about his neck, snapped his 20-gauge together, and issued a challenge to all the grouse in the county to come out and tackle him, either singly or in groups.

It had rained the previous day, and the dogs, full of pep again after their rest, high-tailed it up through the rocky defile which led to the entrance of the cover. We let them range as they chose, so that they might work off some of their keen edge before we came to the first bit of grouse country.

Two hundred yards up the ravine, on a bit of springy ground, we found *Jack* frozen on a solid point, with my youngster backing him beautifully. Apparently they had passed the bird before they caught the scent, for they had swung around and were pointing toward the rocky wall which rose sheer and straight before us. It did not seem possible that a grouse would lie before any object which would so seriously impede its getaway, and I was thinking that it must be a belated woodcock. Suddenly however, there came a thunder of wings, and a pair of grouse got up simultaneously from the very base of the cliff. One took off down the pass, just clearing the tops of the boulders, while the other zoomed straight up the almost perpendicular face of the cliff.

The low flying bird was Gene's, so I swung on the other. No one who has not witnessed it would believe that any bird could attain such speed in an almost vertical flight, but this one went up like an arrow shot from a bow. When I touched the trigger I saw the shot strike the cliff at least three feet beneath it.

Yanking the gun straight upward, for the bird was now almost directly overhead, I touched the other trigger. The wings instantly ceased their driving beat, yet so great was the bird's speed that he actually seemed to hurtle upward for another ten feet, then hang there momentarily suspended before it started to fall to earth.

I have sometimes found it necessary to dodge a falling duck, but I do not recall another instance when I have seen a ruffed grouse dropping directly at me from the skies. Standing there beside the old dog, I watched the bird fall, plummet-like toward us. At the last minute I saw that it would miss me by scant inches, and stood my ground.

Then there came a sudden cough from *Jack,* and I looked down to see him spitting out a mouthful of feathers. It had come

"I stopped just in time, Boss."

so close to him that he snapped at it as it went past his nose, and he missed catching it by inches. I laughed at him, and I shall never forget the look he gave me before he picked up the bird and carried it over to his master. Gene took it, looked at it glumly for a moment, then tossed it back to me.

"How about yours?" I asked. "Did you get it?"

"No." He prefaced the simple negative with a concise and sharp phrase, but even then it sounded unnecessarily short. We feel like that when we let one slide away which we might have taken with a slingshot.

Gene, I suppose, was thinking his own bitter thoughts, while I was wondering why it was that, after all the years, I still knew so little about grouse and the men who hunt them. Why should the shyest of all birds lie like a woodcock in a place like that? Why should the same bird, in the thickest cover, get up out of gunshot, land in some place where it had no more than a few scanty bushes for protection, and then insist on being kicked before it would take wing?

And what human weakness is it that causes us to so soon forget a clean, snappy double, yet causes the missing of an easy straight-away to rankle for years? And why, oh why, when a fellow resolves that for this one day he will show the world something in the way of fancy shooting that it will always remember, must he tighten up until he creaks like a rusty hinge?

We worked through the narrow defile and emerged at last in the lower end of the valley. There is a particularly good woodcock corner there; a half acre patch of alders with a birch knoll behind it, and when *Jack* swung into it and came to a skidding halt I was sure that this time he had found one of the little russet fellows.

I voiced my opinion to Gene, and he agreed that I was probably right. We started in, when with a roar of wings and with raucous cacklings, three pheasants hammered up through the alders. Here was something else over which to ponder. Why didn't they ever give us chances like that during the open season? Where do they all hide when a fellow is really looking for them? Why—

"Watch out!" Gene called sharply. "Another point!"

I swung around and, as I did so, a woodcock bounced into the air before me. Now that the season had ended, pheasants and woodcock were thicker than fleas on a dog.

"Whoa! Hold everything! He's nailed something else!"

Through the alders I could make out *Jack* pointing stanchly, and the pup swinging in at the end of a cast which would bring him well in front of his mate. Fearing that he would bump the bird, I was about to halt him, when he slid, with all four feet braced, to a startled halt. He was merely backing, but I felt my heart warm toward him. In another year or two he would not be content to let another dog do all the finding.

"Another d——— pheasant, probably," Gene said. He had scarcely uttered the words when a bird boiled upward through the branches. Not until it had cleared the tops of the alders and had leveled off in its swift flight did either of us realize that we had permitted a grouse to get cleanly away. Neither of us spoke, but we must have been thinking about what we would do to the next one that got up before us, for when one rose an instant later from almost the same spot, we shot at it so closely together that the reports blended into one cavernous *boom*. Feathers flew, and I saw the bird go crashing down directly in front of the pup.

"That's Wild West stuff," Gene said. "Shoot first and talk it over afterward. Did you kill that bird or did I?"

I knew what was coming, for it is a little joke which he originated, and which he practices on someone at least once each season, but I had seen something which told me that, for once, the thing was going to backfire. "I had a clear shot at her," I said, and waited.

"Well, let's leave it to the dog to decide," he said. "Fetch,

Jack, and bring it to the one who killed it. That's fair enough, huh?"

"Perfectly fair," I assured him. Then, reaching down, I took the bird from the pup's mouth, and for once was glad that he had broken shot to retrieve. The old dog dashed ahead, then turned and came back toward me. Thankful for the screening alders, I held the bird out invitingly as he came close. Then I said, "Thank you," in an unnecessarily loud voice, and walked over to Gene, holding the bird in my hand. I smoothed the ruffled feathers, and managed to keep my face straight.

"It's surprising," I said, "how much some dogs know."

I have never seen such another look of chagrin as that which was written on his face. It might be equalled, though, if he chances to read this, for I have never yet told him the truth concerning the episode.

Once more we went on, and came presently to a growth of birches which were interspersed here and there with apple trees and healthy young pines. It was a place which had seldom failed to produce a bird or two, and as we entered it I felt a pleasurable thrill of anticipation. To add to my satisfaction, the pup had settled down and was hunting seriously. The day was pleasantly warm, there were two grouse in my pocket, and when the pup grew suddenly cautious and then pointed into the tangle before me I would not have exchanged places with a king.

"Point!" I called to Gene, who was plodding along a hundred feet to my right. "The pup has nailed one. Get ahead into the clear. I doubt if I can get a shot in this thicket."

As I waited while he wormed his way through to an open position, I watched the pup admiringly. What style! What animation! What rock-like stanchness! And what a clever guy I had been, too, to reach right into a litter of pups and pick out a grouse dog. I threw my shoulders back and eased my hat up from my forehead, for it had grown uncomfortably tight.

The pup's gaze, I thought, was centered on an apple tree before him. Looking at it closely, I saw a limb tremble slightly. There was not enough breeze to cause the movement, and I knew that a grouse was feeding there. Then another limb trembled—and another.

"It's a grouse convention," I thought. "The tree is full of them."

It was a thrilling moment. The pup was animated and intense. I could feel my heart pounding against my ribs. I was sorry that Gene was missing it all, so I spoke to him cautiously.

"I wish you could see this," I said, pridefully. "He's nailed a whole covey of birds."

"Well, kick 'em out then," he said, practically. "What are you waiting for?"

With gun advanced I moved in. The branches still trembled, but there was no sudden thunder of wings. At last I stood beneath the tree and looked up into it. On a sturdy limb, a fat old porcupine sat, biting juicy chunks from an apple it held beneath a forepaw. Above her, three youngsters climbed precariously among the smaller branches. I called Gene over, but he was strangely unimpressed.

"So that's a bird dog, is it?" he asked, as he glanced at the pup who was still pointing rigidly. "Isn't it wonderful, the things which can be accomplished by scientific breeding?"

I took the pup by the collar and led him away. We worked up the valley, and presently *Jack* winded game. Cutting across in front of me, he slowed abruptly and slid into a point. Gene came in rapidly, prepared for business, while I detoured around the dog and hurried ahead, hoping to win a place where I might intercept the bird if Gene failed to take it. I had not quite reached the spot of my choice when I heard the tumult of wings and the snappy report of the 20-gauge.

Instantly thereafter the bird broke into view, making heavy weather of it as it tried to keep afloat. A lone pine, and a clump of stunted birches blocked its path, and into the latter it splashed. With a tremendous beating of wings it somehow managed to secure a footing on a limb, close in beside the trunk.

"That bird was hit and hit hard," Gene said, as he came pushing through the thicket. "I took a handful of feathers out of her, but she managed to keep going."

"You didn't touch her," I lied. "I saw her. She lighted in that birch," and I pointed her out to him.

"She would never stay there like that if she wasn't hit," he declared, rightly. "See how she's braced against the limb, holding herself up."

"She's all right," I kidded him. "Why don't you take a pot shot at her? You might hit her that way."

He told me where I might go, and expressed his willingness to accompany me before he would shoot a sitting bird.

"Well, if you are determined to miss her again, I'll move her for you," I said, and leaning my gun against one of the smaller birches, I gave the tree a vigorous shake.

I would have taken almost any bet that the bird would come tumbling down upon me, but I heard the flutter of its wings, and looked up just in time to see it flash behind the lone pine. It was a hard shot, and Gene missed it cleanly. I marked the bird's course carefully as it planed down through the stunted growth.

Then I picked up my gun and watched Gene with interest. He was walking around in aimless circles and muttering unintelligibly through set lips. "You did hit her the first time, and hard, too," I confessed, deciding that I had carried the joke a bit too far. "I marked her down. Let's go after her."

It was the pup who found her, a hundred yards farther on, lying with her wings outstretched, and as dead as Julius Caesar.

"Five shells, and only one bird," Gene said, as he stowed her away. "I know what the trouble is, though. I've been hurrying too much. I'll take my time on the next one."

That was the cue for me to watch my step, but I muffed it and we went on. As we were crossing another birch ridge the dogs found game. We went up to them, side by side, and were well up to the dogs when a pair of grouse went boiling out, straight away. The setup was so perfect that there was no need for haste, and I was swinging leisurely at the one on my side when Gene's gun barked once—twice—and both birds came tumbling down.

"That proves what I was saying about hurrying," he said. "I took my time on that pair." I don't know why I ever try to razz him, for it always works out thus in the end. But I do know the reason for that. He's a better man than I am.

A few hundred yards farther on, the pup, going gloriously now, bumped a whole covey of birds. We could hear them getting up, one after another, in heart-warming numbers. Immediately the youngster came in, looking shame-faced for what he had done, but he redeemed himself shortly afterward by nailing a single in a tangle of blackberry vines.

Until then, the birds had been lying remarkably well, but this one ran like a turkey. The pup was plainly puzzled whenever the scent vanished, but I urged him on and he picked it up from time to time. Working with him, trying to make him go ahead confidently and boldly, we finally forced the bird into a corner where it decided to lie. But when I put it up it burst out before Gene's face, and he stood, with his gun under his arm, and let it go, unruffled upon its way.

"Too easy," he explained, when I looked at him questioningly. "I'm not going to carry the limit around all the rest of the day, with nothing to look forward to. I want to enjoy life."

One by one, the dogs located the scattered birds, but as though Gene's refusal of his chance had brought us bad luck, they invariably got up well out of range. Leaving them at last, we went up through the remainder of the cover without securing a point.

We ate lunch beside a clear, cool spring, rested for half an hour as a mark of respect to the rugged trail we had trod, then started back down the other side of the valley. Almost immediately we began to find birds, but it was almost unbelievable that they could have so changed their tactics since morning. The pup was wholly outclassed, while even the older dog seemed to grow slightly bewildered by the unvarying sameness of their routine. *"Point,"* one of us would call, and *Whir-r-r-r* would go a bird from somewhere in the distance. A moment later we would see it go scaling far up the side of the cliffs where we could not follow.

"They've learned their lesson," Gene said when, some three hours later, having neared the lower end of the valley, we paused to look at each other questioningly. "It didn't take 'em long either. Well, five birds are enough. Let's go home."

I agreed. We turned—and there were the dogs before us, side by side, and each stretching into that intoxicating scent until he looked to be at least ten feet long. The grouse must have been lying almost within tasting distance of them, for when I swung the gun around and took a step in their direction it boiled up from under their very noses. I cut it down, and at the report we could hear birds thundering up in the woods before us.

"Listen to 'em go," Gene exclaimed. "Don't that sound like old times?"

It did. It sounded great. I know no sweeter music than the booming roar of their startled flight, and I know of nothing else which will set my heart to pounding so ecstatically. I love to hunt them. I like to bag a few of them occasionally. But better still I like to know that despite drought and flood, disease and pestilence, vermin, predators, automobiles and man, the ruffed grouse has the fortitude to survive and periodically replenish our woodlands with others of its kind.

I was thinking some such thoughts when the pup came up with the bird. I smoothed the mottled feathers, felt the plump weight of the breast, and looked up to see Gene hurrying off to where a spot of white proclaimed that *Jack* had found another.

How spitefully a 20-gauge can bark in a wooded valley when the sun has slid down behind the mountains and the wind is stilled. Gene came back with the bird in his hand, and a look of utter contentment on his face. Who would care to be a millionaire if he could never know that feeling?

Five minutes later, the pup stuck his nose in the air and went to his bird as a grouse dog should. I stole up to him, ran a hand

A dog will find most of the cripples.

down his quivering back, then straightened and took another forward step.

It happened as I knew it was bound to do. No day like this could be marred at the last moment. It was foreordained. It was written in the stars. Straight toward the western sky the grouse zoomed, bulking huge, and outlined with cameo clearness against the soft crimson. I pressed the trigger, broke the gun, tossed away the empty shell and dropped the other one in my pocket. The pup was standing with lifted head, his ears cocked forward, listening.

"All right," I said. "Go fetch."

CHAPTER 4

Red-Letter Day

I doubt if old man Noah and I could ever have hit it off very well together. We would have been friends of a sort, I imagine, but never palsy-walsy, for we would have split on one big issue.

The main reason why we could not have amalgamated is because he wasn't a bird hunter. A fisherman, maybe, but I'll bet my pile he didn't care a rap about grouse shooting. If he had cared, he wouldn't have been so happy when it rained. Oh, he was happy, all right, for he had been waiting years for it. I imagine that when it started to sprinkle he grinned, spat over the rail and said "Whoopee, boys! Here she comes!"

Unless he is a fisherman or a duck hunter, a guy like that ain't human. If he had been obliged to swab out the old scatter-gun twice a day to keep it from rusting, and had been cooped up with a pair of young bird dogs that were full of thunder and lightning and just rarin' to go, you can mark my words he would have sung a different tune. I don't know what he would have said, but I have a very good idea how he would have said it. He might have held it in for a time, but after a few days of incessant rain he would have hauled off and cut loose, with the result that instead of being canonized he would have been excommunicated.

I'm in favor of rain in October. A brisk little shower one or two nights a week suits me fine; but when someone opens the spigot and lets it run for five straight days right in the middle of the grouse season, why, there ought to be a law.

That's what happened last year. It had been hot and dry for the first two weeks of the season, and then along about the mid-

dle of the month it rained. Just an average sort of downpour at
first, but the skies kept growing darker, and then it settled down
to business and rained and rained and rained.

Within the house everything grew clammy to the touch. Boots
mildewed, moisture fogged the window panes, and all varnished
surfaces were like so much sticky fly-paper. The shells, rescued
from the basement and stored upon the kitchen mantle, continued to swell until one could count the wads through the
cases. The dogs, philosophical about it at first, grew daily more
despondent, lay behind the range and peered out at me with
melancholy and accusing eyes.

Then, at the end of the fifth day, when my vocabulary was
exhausted and reason was tottering on its throne, the clouds
parted and a setting sun looked down upon a clean and newly
washed world.

I knew, even as Gene climbed into the car the next morning,
that this was going to be a red-letter day. The long rain had not
only kept hunters from the woods and given the birds an opportunity to get together again, but it had also brought about scenting conditions which should be ideal. The sun, rising in a
cloudless sky, would toll the grouse out into the openings where
shooting would be easy. The dogs, rested and eager, would show
us something in the way of style and form and bird hunting
ability that we would long remember. Such is the stuff of which
dreams are made.

Twenty miles from home, we turned the dogs loose in the
Topham cover, and almost immediately learned that we had
erred in our judgment concerning scenting conditions. Instead of having been cleansed and freshened by the rain, the
earth had a sour and musty smell that baffled even good old *Bob*.
With the gentlest of breezes to aid him, he still bumped a single
that was feeding in a thorn-plum thicket, and repeated the offense a few minutes later on another one that thundered out
from behind a low-growing hemlock.

That was bad enough, but when Gene's *Rap*, an irrepressible youngster in whom the fires of youth flamed high, went free-wheeling down through the cover and put up a covey of birds that scattered like chaff before the wind of his approach, I began to suspect that the day might not assume the vermilion tones in which my fancy had pictured it.

The sun rode higher, shining with unseasonable warmth, and the ground began to steam beneath the hot rays. *Rap*, ashamed of his mistakes, worked cautiously—too cautiously—for he hesitated on the scent of a close lying bird, and when I went boldly in, believing that it lay some distance farther on, I missed it cleanly as it roared out from almost between my feet.

I have hunted grouse in all sorts of places and under all sorts of conditions, and I boldly assert that the greatest handicap a grouse hunter is ever called upon to face is a mental one. There are but few men who are physically incapable of pointing a gun so that an occasional hit may be scored unless something goes wrong with their thinking aparatus; but I know to my great sorrow that many a minor thing may so ball up the works of that intricate machine that it will misfire in every cylinder.

It was so on this occasion. There was no reason why a bit of sloppy work on the part of the dogs, and an amateurish miss on my part should rattle me, but it did. There was no sane reason why Gene should become infected also, for he is of the steady and unruffled type, but evidently the thing was as contagious as smallpox, for he missed an easy cross-shot which he could ordinarily have taken with one hand, and then let another slide unharmed through a salvo which sounded like a 21-gun salute to an admiral.

It was natural that such an exhibition would exert no steadying influence upon the dogs, and their behavior—which had been bad enough at the start—became steadily worse. There seemed to be no limit to the errors we all made, and neither did there seem to be any way to stop them.

Gene, even more taciturn than usual, went grimly ahead, resolved, I suppose, to put an end to the whole silly business, but it was he who finally called a halt. He seldom wastes a word, and on this occasion he ran absolutely true to form. In a few well chosen and forceful sentences he expressed his opinion of the dogs, the birds, the cover, himself and me. I listened carefully, for it was my wish to supplement his observations if he omitted anything, but there was no need. It was a summary remarkable for its exactness.

"Let's go home," I suggested. "Let's go home and stay there until we grow up."

"Let's go down to the schoolhouse cover," he said, "and cut out all this foolishness."

We drove down to the little red schoolhouse, one of the pitiful survivors of its kind, and parked the car just beyond the grassless, hard packed yard. From within came the drone of voices, the listless monotone of prisoners confined upon that glorious October day. My watch proclaimed the hour to be half after eleven.

"Let's eat," Gene said. We dug the lunch kit from the confusion of guns and shells and dogs, and poured steaming coffee from the vacuum jug. Just as we were packing the things away a bell tinkled somewhere inside the gloomy walls, the door burst open, and children erupted from it like lava from a particularly active volcano.

A freckled, red-headed youngster of twelve, and an overalled towhead of similar years paused when they saw the car and came diffidently over. My mind leaped back across the years and I knew what it was that drew them so irresistibly toward us. Not Gene's grim visage or my witless stare. No, it was the eager faces of the dogs, thrust out from the open windows, and the knowledge that a pair of guns reposed within the car that was the lodestone.

The redhead aired his knowledge to the towhead. "The white

one's a setter," I heard him say. "The brown-and-white one is a pointer."

I smiled in an effort to convince them that we were harmless, said "Hello," and watched while they drew closer.

"Didja get anything?" the towhead asked.

Gene's explosive "No" almost lost them to us; but they came back when we climbed out and slipped the guns from their cases. Once more I remembered the days of my youth. "We're going down there in the hollow," I said. "Would you like to tag along?"

After all, it isn't hard to win friends. I gained two as easily as that. We struck off through the birch and alder run, and almost immediately *Rap,* Gene's pointer, nailed a bird, while my setter, *Bob,* backed him beautifully. It was a picture worthy of a place in any gallery, and as I felt the thrill of its beauty tingling in my veins after all the years, I thought how much more thrilling it must be to those youngsters who whispered so excitedly behind us.

It was Gene, edging cautiously around the dogs, who got the shot, and as the bird came rocketing up through the alders he wiped it out with a fast and flawless swing. His effortless speed has long since become an old story to me, but I knew it must seem like black magic to the boys. They crowded in when *Rap* came out with the bird, and gloated over it and smoothed its mottled feathers when Gene tossed it over for them to carry.

We went on, and immediately the pointer again began making game. With head held high and his tail vibrating like a rattler's, he cut diagonally across the gully and came to a stand close to a clump of pines that stood upon the higher ground. It was probable that the bird would break through the pines, so I hurried around them hoping to get a shot if it flushed beyond Gene's range, and left matters in his hands. An instant later I heard the beat of startled wings, the sharp crash of the gun and the thud of the bird as it crashed to earth. I went back. The boys' eyes were protruding like doorknobs.

"Gee!" the redhead said. "He can shoot, can't he!"

"He ought to be able to," I said. "Did you ever hear of Buffalo Bill?"

The bulging eyes protruded farther. "Gee, yes!"

"Well, that's his brother," I told them, in a confidential whisper. "He's Pa'tridge Bill. Yes, sir! Good old Pa'tridge Bill, who hits 'em where they ain't."

There was something of both awe and reverence in the look they bestowed on Gene's retreating back, and I knew that in their eyes, at least, he would always rank with the immortals, but when I noticed that they were looking questioningly at me I hurried on. Remembering the morning, I was not yet ready to classify myself.

Up above me, in the thin fringe of brush which bordered the gully, I caught a flash of something white, and presently the setter came into an opening, trailing a running bird as he knew so well how to do. It was evident that this grouse was no novice at the game we were playing, and was heading for some dense thicket behind which it could take off in safety. It was my job to outguess it if I could.

Cutting rapidly ahead to turn it toward the more open country, I saw that Gene was hurrying up to my assistance. Still the grouse refused to fly, and at last, if the setter's rolling eyes could be relied upon, it lay directly between us. I took one more step and it came out low and fast. I swung on it, but Gene beat me to the shot. A puff of feathers floated in the air as the bird nose-dived into the alders.

"Gee! Three!" the towhead exclaimed, in what may possibly be the shortest tone poem ever uttered. Gene's stock which had already gone above par was still pyramiding skyward, while mine which had started at zero had fallen several points.

We went on once more, an imposing safari, with the dogs

scouting before us, and the native game-bearers bringing up the rear. Presently the gully narrowed and we knew we were nearing its end. Beyond us lay a bare, rock-studded pasture in which no self-respecting grouse would feed.

Well, the cover had held its quota, for it was seldom that we ever found more than three in it. We could come back in a few days, though, and find as many more that had worked up from the swamp into which the gully poured its spring floods.

When we had almost reached the end, the dogs, swinging in toward each other from opposite sides of the run, slid simultaneously into rigid points. They were thirty yards away, but even as we turned toward them a grouse came up from between them, soared up to the top of the bank and swung around on a course which would bring it past me at a distance of at least forty yards.

It was a long shot. Too long, but the bird was silhouetted sharply against the skyline, without so much as a hindering twig between us. I swung well ahead of it and touched the trigger. I like to see them crumple as that one did, dead in mid-air. Head down, it crashed to earth and the setter bore it proudly back to me.

Gene's comment, "You strained the gun on that one," was not complimentary, for he does not approve of taking long shots, and neither do I, as a rule. It results in too many crippled birds. Nevertheless, this was a clean kill, and the boys appreciated it. There was just a hint of respect in the glance they gave me. They didn't place me in the same class with old Pa'tridge Bill, but by their whispered conversation I knew they thought I at least had possibilities.

Ah, me! How highly we prize the laurel wreath! What a disappointment it was to know that these youngsters whom I had never seen before, and would probably never see again, would always think of me as a chap who was only one-third as good as their idol. I would have welcomed an opportunity to disprove the libel, but at that moment I caught the distant tinkle of the school bell and knew that we had come to the parting of the ways. The boys looked a each other guiltily and then held another whispered conversation.

I said, "You're late, boys. You'd better hurry back."

They had no verbal answer for that but their eyes were eloquent. The schoolhouse was close and stuffy, and this was one of those glorious October days when all nature called. My mind leaped back across the years to another similar building from whose windows I gazed like a convict from behind prison bars. I remembered that a well rounded education cannot be gleaned from text books alone, and that there are a multitude of things which every boy should know that no sharp-nosed, bespectacled spinster can teach him.

"Do you know where there are any more birds?" I asked.

They knew. Trust any out-of-doors boy to know where every trout lurks in the brooks he fishes, and the haunts of all the game within his private domain. There was a birch run, they said, just beyond the pasture, and in it were four more pa'tridge. I looked at Gene. He nodded approval and we started off.

The run was a sweetheart. In the moist ground in its center a thread of alders grew, while on either side the gentle slopes were covered with clean, straight birches. It was grouse country in any man's land, and just the sort of place a flight woodcock would choose for a quick lunch. We would look it over some later day on the full of the moon.

Gene swung over to the right beyond the alders, and my last shred of egotism departed when I saw both boys edge away to follow him. They would have been gone in another instant if the setter had not chosen that moment to stretch out in one of his statuesque points. Their loyalty to Gene was unquestioned, but they came back to follow me as I went up to the dog.

He had the bird nailed solidly. That it was lying close I could tell by the way he braced back with his forelegs, as though his nose was an inch over the danger line, and by his eyes, which rolled beseechingly back at me as I came up.

I was within ten feet of him when two grouse exploded from a fern clump and zoomed straight up to clear the tops of the birches. Not often do such chances for a double come to a grouse hunter, and they occur with less frequency each passing year. I took the first one before it reached the tops of the birches, and crumpled the other one an instant later.

From behind me came twin and incredulous gasps from the boys. This was the sort of education they could not get inside a schoolroom, and I felt less guilty about being the direct cause of their playing hookey.

"Didja see that?" the redhead exclaimed. "*Bing-bing*, and he killed 'em both."

With the dog working ahead, I went up through the birches, and such is the fickleness of public opinion, and so readily are new heroes crowned, that Gene found himself a cast-off idol, while it was I upon whom the gaping populace stared. Gene, however, is one of those phlegmatic chaps to whom the plaudits of the world mean nothing—at least during the grouse season. His one thought then is to find grouse, and he was still running true to form.

Off to the right I heard his "Steady, boy," and then the snare-drum roll that was cut short by the echoing crash of his gun. Presently he came over to my side of the run, with his fourth bird in his hand and a look of utter contentment on his face.

"Well, that's that," he said. "It was fun while it lasted." He opened his gun, extracted the shells and swung in behind me. "You've one to go. I'll look over your shoulder and tell you how you happened to miss."

Two hundred yards farther on the setter once more winded game. Straight and true, with head held high, he went in and came to a point close to a tumble-down wall that marked an ancient boundary. As though it were a hurdle which they could not surmount, the birches stopped there. Beyond the wall, a tangle of spruce and hemlock grew.

As I came up to the dog a grouse roared out of the last fringe of birches and headed, low down, for the safe shelter of the evergreens. The distance it had to travel was not more than thirty feet, and it is surprising how quickly a thoroughly frightened ruffed grouse can cover so brief a span. It is even more surprising how fast a very ordinary wing shot can go into action.

The bird was still a yard from that protective screen when my shot charge overtook it, and as it smashed into the green canopy I could see its outline perfectly, a deadly circle in which the stricken bird formed its geometrical center. It was one of those instinctive, split-second shots which I miss far too often, but which thrills me from toes to fingertips when I connect. It must have impressed the boys, too, for the redhead asked me—and there was something like awe in his voice—"What do they call you?"

I didn't understand his meaning. "What do they call me?" I repeated.

"Yeah. You said he was Pa'tridge Bill. Who are you?"

"Oh," I said. "Why, I'm the fellow who is teaching him how to shoot."

When the bird was retrieved I tossed it over to the boys. Equally burdened now with four each, they looked not unlike two young gentlemen of color emerging from a chicken coop in the wee small hours, but it was apparent that they were not yet satisfied, for they looked questioningly at us as we called the dogs in and headed for the car.

"There are more birds up beyond the spruces," the towhead volunteered.

"Yeah?" said Gene. "Well, what of it?"

"Ain't you going to hunt any more?"

"The limit," I explained, "is four birds each, and we have them."

The boy hesitated, then muttered, "Nobody would know."

Gene picked it up instantly, before I could frame a reply. "You would know," he said, "and so would we. It's only once or twice in a season that we take the limit, and it has been five years since we took them as quickly as this. You don't think we would spoil this day by trying to take more birds, do you?"

Proof of the pudding. Gyp, four birds and the old reliable Parker.

He said it decisively, and I added nothing to temper the rebuke, for this, too, was something the text books should teach, and do not.

We climbed the bank and struck off across the pasture, but when we came within sight of the schoolhouse the boys hesitated. This, it seemed, was the deadline. Playing hookey had its inevitable consequences, as I well remembered, and the boys preferred to postpone the affair until the morrow.

We stowed the birds in our pockets, said goodbye to the boys and left them standing there, watching us, and looking a little wistfully, I thought, into the years which lay just ahead.

"What time is it?" Gene asked, when we reached the car.

I looked at my watch. "It's two o'clock exactly."

"Eight birds," he said, "in two hours. Not bad. Not bad at all."

"I'm glad the kids went along," I said. "It's nice for them to have an idol to cherish."

"If you want to be glad about something," he said, "you can be damned glad they weren't with us this morning."

CHAPTER 5

Last Day

Old Bill drew a long breath and hoped it would ease the guilty feeling that was tightening things up in his chest, but it didn't help. In fact, it made him feel worse. No matter how much a fellow needed the money, selling a dog that had been with you every day for four years was something to turn any man's stomach.

It was different from selling a litter of pups. You knew they were young enough to forget you in a few days. Selling *Jack* was a different story. *Jack* wouldn't forget.

He looked down at the pointer and it was as though someone had put a wrench on his insides and given it a twist. They didn't turn out dogs like this every day. Standing there with the sun striking splashes of light from his liver-and-white coat, *Jack* looked like the champion Bill knew him to be.

That was the frightening part of it, now that the moment had come. If the dog were only a second rater, so that some of the others would show him up, everything would work out all right, but Bill knew there wasn't a chance of that happening. He wasn't kidding himself either, the way lots of hunters did about their dogs, seeing only their good qualities, and blind as a bat when it came to noticing their faults. No, Bill wasn't kidding himself.

You could spend the whole hunting season, going up and down the state from the Canadian border to salt water, and you wouldn't find a bird dog anywhere that could hold a candle to *Jack*. A big, bold dog, with stamina enough to go eight hours a day and seven days a week, yet wise enough to slow his pace

65

without command and hunt to gun in thick cover. He had a chokebore nose that could wind a grouse at a hundred yards, and he had an uncanny way of going boldly in on them to the last tricky inch, and nailing them there with the accuracy of a magnetic compass.

Those were the things that old Bill knew, and because he knew them he was uneasy. Standing there, waiting for the starter's signal, he wished there was some way he could back out. Within him was a sure conviction that his dog was going to take this heat. His brace mate, an undersized setter, straining at the leash which the tall stranger held so confidently, didn't have what it takes to win a field trial. A blind man could tell she wasn't in the pointer's class. *Jack* would win this heat, and tomorrow they would put him down with another winner. After that would come the finals, and the finals were what Bill dreaded.

He chuckled whimsically at the thought. He'd bet that some of these men would give a thousand dollars to see their dog win, and he would give a thousand dollars to lose. Yes, sir, he'd give a thousand dollars gladly—if he had it. That was where the rub came. If he had a thousand dollars he wouldn't be up here trying to win a cup so he could sell the dog who won it. That was a low-down trick, but there wasn't any other way out. He didn't blame the bank people—not much—although he did think Mr. Burgess might have given him a little more time. Another year, say. They wouldn't lose anything except the interest, and that didn't amount to a great lot on six hundred dollars.

Crops were bound to be better next season. But there wasn't any use to think about that now. Mr. Burgess had put it plain enough. The interest hadn't been paid for three years and, to protect itself, the bank would have to take over. There weren't any holes a fellow could wriggle through—except one. If he went in and slapped the six hundred, together with the three years interest, down on the counter, that would end it and the place would still be his.

There was only one fault to be found with that plan. It wouldn't be the same place—not unless the dog was there. Bill didn't like to think about the lonely nights and the days of wandering around the farm, looking back every few steps for a dog that would never again come swinging along at heel. It was a clear September day, but for a moment everything blurred as though a fog had blown across the course. Bill cleared his throat noisily.

"Nervous?" the man with the setter asked.

"You named it," Bill said. "I'm as jittery as a girl settin' up with her first beau."

"Take it easy," the stranger counseled. "There's nothing to it, really. Keep your dog as nearly on the course as you can, and trust to luck. We can't all win."

"No," said Bill. "I've been thinkin' about that. Somebody's got to lose." But while he was saying it he was thinking how glad he'd be to swap chances with the fellow. All *he* stood to lose was a cup that was probably plated. After it was all over he would still have his dog. There wouldn't be anybody coming up to him and asking, "What's your price on him, brother?" And even if they did ask, the fellow could still tell them to go to hell.

The stranger straightened suddenly and his gloved hand grew tense on the leash. "Here's the starter," he said.

Bill's glance swept upward to the horseshoe that rimmed the course, and he could feel the tenseness of the gallery. Dog-men. Two hundred of them, staring down at the two waiting dogs. In that moment Bill forgot all the troubles that perplexed his soul. The men who waited there were his kind of people, drawn, some of them, for hundreds of miles in the hope that at least one entry would run a heat of championship caliber. Well, they would see it today if they had never seen it before.

Bill stooped above the dog. "Just remember that it's pheasants you're huntin', instead of grouse. Some of 'em will lie right under your nose, and others will run like turkeys, but you just do your best and we'll show 'em somethin'."

He was stooping there, whispering, when the starter's voice asked, "Are you ready, gentlemen?"

Bill's mouth was too dry to answer, but he waved his free hand in an affirmative gesture, unhooked the snap and held the pointer there by crooking a finger under the collar.

"Then let them go."

It is good, that first moment when a pair of bird dogs are unleashed at a field trial. Fresh, eager, they sweep out in a great burst of speed, in an effort each to determine the other's metal.

As the pointer leaped away, Bill could hear the exhalation of many breaths behind him, and something glowed within him as he watched the dogs. The setter he had rightly judged to be a flash in the pan, without the stamina to go the whole period, but he had not guessed there was so much speed concealed in its slender frame. It went toward the distant cover like a flash of light, yet neck and neck with it the pointer eased along in a deceptive and effortless stride.

Only for a moment, though. A hundred yards out, the pointer braced his feet, reversed ends and came to a clawing, skidding stop. Then boldly, confidently, with head held high, it roaded a dozen steps to the right and froze into immobility.

"Ah!" That was the gallery, and Bill grinned as he looked around for the judges. They came at his call of "Point," riding up from the edge of the wood where they had been sitting their horses, and drew to a halt as Bill stepped in front of his dog.

The bird lay in a weed tangle, crouching close to earth, but when Bill kicked a matted clump it came out noisily, hammering out and up on frightened wings.

There's a test for your dog, mister. When the tense silence is shattered by a startled bird whose flailing pinions set the leaves dancing and fill the air with their thunder. When every instinct in your dog cries out to it to spring upon its quarry. When, with every nerve aquiver, it still stands there immovable, like a thing carved from marble, you've done your work well. You've got a dog that is *stanch*.

Old Bill knew his dog and, because he knew him so well, he was guilty of a bit of play acting then. As the bird thundered out of the tangle he did not glance at the dog or give him a steadying word. Instead, he discharged the pistol the secretary had loaned him, then watched the pheasant go winging across the flatland and disappear in the thick cover beyond. Not until then did he turn back to the pointer who was still standing rigidly, and from the tail of his eye he caught a nod of approval from one of the judges.

With his mind occupied with what lay before, he waved the dog on and was swinging into his stride behind him, when he stopped and looked sharply back at the judges.

"Doggone!" he said. "That's Mr. Burgess!"

For a moment he forgot about field trials as his half formed resentment against the banker stirred anew within him. Try as he might, he could not rid himself of the conviction that the man up there on the horse could have been more lenient had he chosen to do so, and because he felt that way it was easy to suppose that the other also had a personal feeling in the matter. He wondered what effect it would have upon the moment when they picked the winner. Would the financier be influenced by what his eyes saw, or by the feeling he had in his heart? Bill began to fret about it, for now that he had made up his mind he couldn't afford to lose.

He might have saved himself three days of needless worry, for on the last afternoon, at the end of a heat which had the gallery up on their toes with excitement, it was the banker's nod that gave the cup to the pointer. Later, when Bill was piling his duffel into the battered old flivver, he looked up to see Mr. Burgess standing beside him.

"You have a great dog there," the banker said. "What's your price on him?"

With a caution born of years of experience, Bill hedged. "I don't exactly know," he said. "I've been looking for one like him for forty years. They don't happen much oftener than that, I guess. Chances are, I'll never find another one. You probably wouldn't want to pay what he's worth."

"Probably not," the banker agreed. "Still, if he can handle grouse as well as he handles pheasants, I might be interested."

Bill said, "Mister, unless you've seen this one handle 'em, you ain't never seen a grouse dog."

"How about next Sunday? Do you want to go out and prove it?" asked Mr. Burgess.

"Any day in the week," Bill said. "You come along up."

The banker, Bill thought, was about the poorest shot he had ever run up against. Lumbering through the cover like an armored tank, and blazing away haphazardly at every bird that fluttered a feather, he was enough to unnerve any dog, but the pointer didn't seem to mind. Except for a puzzled stare at each miss, he went serenely upon his way, a master craftsman absorbed in his work, and nailing bird after bird with uncanny accuracy. For two hours the banker followed him: then he called for a halt. "I've seen enough," he said. "He has more stuff than any dog I've ever hunted over. What is your price?"

Bill's throat felt dry. He had known it was going to be hard, but he had not guessed it was going to hurt like this. He knew he ought to look the fellow straight in the eye, just as though he didn't give a damn whether he bought or not, and say, "He's a real one, mister, and the real ones cost real money. It's goin' to cost any man just a thousand bucks to walk off with this dog."

That was the way to put it to him. Then he could take it or

leave it—only he wouldn't leave it. He'd leave the thousand instead, and that would leave Bill sitting pretty. He could square things up at the bank and have enough left over to buy seed next spring. Then, by digging into work and forgetting about dogs and hunting he'd make a go of it.

Yes, that was the thing to do. Just forget that the dog was the only companion he had left, set a price on him and get it over with. He opened his mouth to speak, and surprised himself by saying, "I don't believe I want to sell him, Mr. Burgess.

"Not sell him?" The banker's tone was testy. "Come, come! I don't want to press you, but there is your obligation to the bank. How will you take care of that?"

"I don't know exactly, but ——

"Of course you don't know. You can't pay it. Now here's what I'll do. I'll take care of the note and give you a hundred beside. How does that appeal to you?"

"It doesn't," Bill informed him. "If ever a bird dog was worth a thousand dollars, this one is. I wouldn't take a cent less."

"You're a tough old bird." The banker said it without malice. "All right. I'll make it an even thousand."

There it was, the offer Bill had known would surely come, and to it there could be but one reply: "You've bought a bird dog, mister." That was the answer, and no one knew it better than Bill, yet he could not frame the words. Instead, he said, haltingly, "I—I'll think it over and let you know in a day or two. It's—well—it's kind of hard to—" He choked and turned his head away.

"I know." Mr. Burgess' tone was mildly sympathetic. "I know. It's tough, but it's only a dog. You drop into the bank in a few days and we'll fix everything up."

With his hat pulled down to shield his eyes from the newly risen sun, old Bill sat on the frosty pine steps and looked out over the tired land. Beside him, the liver-and-white pointer crowded over so that his shoulder crowded hard against Bill's knee, while on the worn treads the hard tail set up a rythmic drumming.

"Cut out the shovin'," Bill said. "Ain't you got no sense this mornin'? No, of course you haven't. Couldn't expect you to, bein' my dog. I'm the biggest fool in the state. You ought to be ashamed even to be seen with me, let alone shinin' up to me that way."

The pointer laid his square muzzle across the man's knee. Bill's hand went out automatically, but he checked it and pushed it deep into his coat pocket.

"Beggar," he said. "You ain't hungry, but you're apt to be. Yes, sir, if you stick around me you're likely to be honest-to-God hungry from now on. The bank's run us into a corner. If we set still they'll potshot us, and if we flush they'll let us have both barrels. They've got us either way. I can't see no hole we can crawl through."

He let his gaze wander out across the frost-browned fields to the stunted corn that had not been worth the harvesting. "Run down," he said, and turned his head so that he could see the barn. It, too, was a weathered gray, and the roof showed patches where the shingles had blown away. "Run down," he repeated. "That's the trouble with everything around here. I'm sixty years old, and it looks like I was run-down too. Run-down or washed-up, whatever you've a mind to call it."

"That's what comes of being a fool. Do you know what I did? I turned Mr. Burgess down. Yes, I did. He offered me a thousand dollars for your homely hide, and yesterday I went down there to get it. But I didn't. No, sir. Instead, I told them where to go. There! Now you know what sort of fool you're chummin' round with. Go on! Beat it! Go find somebody who's got some brains and be his dog."

The pointer snuggled closer.

"Dog-gone it!" Bill said. "Don't you understand what I'm

tellin' you? If you was his dog you could have cake every night for supper, but if you stick with me you'll be lucky if you get a secondhand bone to chew on. The bank's takin' the place over tomorrow, and we ain't got nothin' left. Not a thing." The pointer pushed his head beneath Bill's arm. Bill shut his eyes tight. "Except each other," he added.

Some minutes later, he said, "The way I figger it, it's goin' to be kinda cold sleepin' under a fence here this winter, but if we were down South it wouldn't be so bad. It looks to me as though there ought to be a place there somewhere where a fellow could earn his keep exercisin' dogs. If we could just make out to get down there I'd take a chance on gettin' the job, but there ain't much left that we've got a right to sell. Mr. Burgess was pretty strict about that. He was peeved, I guess.

"I could maybe scrape up a little, but the bus fare and the express on you would come to about forty dollars." Old Bill sighed wistfully. "I wish there was some way we could make it. I know what you can do on grouse, but I've sure got a hankering to see you road into a bunch of quail. Make you look foolish, I'll bet." He pulled a silken ear fondly. "Yes, sir, it takes a real dog to handle those babies."

Sitting there on the worn steps, Bill reviewed the parade of years that had passed since Mary died. Something in Bill had died that night too, and he had drifted since. He realized it, now that it was too late. When the going got tough he should have dug in a little harder: a fellow had to provide for his old age.

Sixty years had brought him over a long road, but now he was nearing its end. When a fellow got to be that age there wasn't much chance of his starting over again.

"Well, we've got to do something," he said. "We can't just sit here and starve." The wind stirred again, bringing with it the crisp tang of the woodlands, and as Bill sniffed it he unconsciously threw his shoulders back. Today was the last day. The last day of grace at the bank, and the last day of open season on grouse. A lump arose in his throat when he thought that it was possible he would never see another New England autumn.

He paused irresolutely as a sudden impulse seized him, then said aggressively; "Well, boy, we're goin' to have this day anyway. That'll be one more they can't take away from us." He went into the house and came out presently, a pump gun cradled beneath his arm, his hands thrust into the pockets of his coat to count the shells. "Nine," he said. "We'll have to be careful not to waste any."

The pointer dashed and danced around him Then, at a motion of the man's hand he struck off across the fields, moving as easily and as effortlessly as a swallow.

"A good dog," Bill said, approvingly, and holding the gun upright in one hand he pressed the release and watched the action slide all the way to the bottom and stop with a muffled click. "And a good gun," he added. It had cost him a hundred and forty dollars, but he had never regretted it, for he had an artisan's satisfaction in using good tools.

Crossing the brown fields, Bill climbed the stone wall that surrounded the rocky pasture. Through the low blueberry bushes the pointer held his pace, and on through the open growth of hardwood, but when they came to the birch side hill he slowed abruptly.

"You'd better slow down, you nitwitted old hard-head," Bill said, affectionately. "High-tailin' it around that way. I was about ready to whale the tar out of you."

With his head cocked on one side and one ear lifted, the pointer looked at him, then turned and went on, but his stride had shortened until a man could easily keep him in sight as he quartered back and forth.

"And I didn't have to teach him to do it," Bill said to himself. "He's just a natural born gun dog." He dropped a shell into the gun's chamber, closed the action and slid two more into the magazine. Then he went on after the dog.

They had not progressed fifty yards when the pointer slowed abruptly, took several infinitely cautious steps, then halted. As he stood there with his whole body rigid, his head swung slowly to the right as though it were drawn by some irresistible force. Then his muzzle tipped slightly downward and all movement ceased.

"That's nailin' 'em," Bill said, approvingly, and slid the gun from under his arm. As he went in, he thought how infallibly accurate the pointer was in locating his birds. "I could sight the gun over his nose and blow that bird to kingdom come."

The grouse came out on thundering wings, vaulting up through the birches like a rocket. The butt of the gun touched Bill's shoulder and cradled there with a sure firmness that brought the comb hard against his cheek at the precise instant the bird reached the tops of the trees. The crash of nitro woke the startled echoes, and for a moment the bird hung motionless against the cobalt sky ere it came crashing down.

"Nice work," Bill said, when the pointer came proudly in with the bird.

A quarter mile ahead, near a dry stump, the dog paused momentarily, then lifted his head and went angling off into the wind. Coming up to the stump, Bill saw that the finely powdered soil had been recently disturbed. "They've been dustin' here," he said, and hurried after the dog.

A short gunshot away, the pointer was still moving forward, but there was a new caution in his bearing. His legs had assumed a grotesque rigidity, seeming to move only at shoulder and hip as he eased his feet carefully down.

"She's movin'," Bill said, and forgot everything else in the keen delight he always felt in watching a good dog handle a wary, running bird.

For a score of yards farther the pointer went, with head held high and nose outthrust, and as he went ahead he quartered slightly to left or right as the need arose, in order that he might keep exactly in the center of that thread of scent. Entranced, Bill followed until the pointer, in the act of taking another forward step, paused abruptly, balancing himself on three legs.

Bill stepped ahead, and like a bolt from the blue a grouse

Late in the season a good man with a duck gun can
score on the long shots.

went rocketing away, twisting in and out among the gray tree trunks, but it had not traveled thirty feet before disaster overtook it. The wings went suddenly limp and the bird bounced as it hit the ground.

Higher up on the hillside, Bill went guardedly in behind another point, but as he neared the dog two birds flushed from a spot some thirty yards to one side. He swung toward the sound, with the gun at his shoulder, but he knew before he saw them that the birds were too far away.

"You kinda slipped up on that pair, I reckon," he said to the pointer, and even as he spoke a grouse flushed from a spot not more than twenty feet from the dog's nose.

Bill hurried then. The bird was within a scant foot of a screening clump of evergreen when the charge overtook it. For a moment it hung suspended on banked pinions, then went hammering down through the branches.

"I beg your pardon," Bill said humbly. "I guess I'll never get used to owning a dog like you. You ain't lied to me since the Lord knows when, but I can't get over the habit of thinkin' I know more than you do."

The pointer grinned at him, then went in after the bird, but when Bill had stowed it away, instead of starting off again, he looked questioningly up into the man's face.

"Darned if I don't believe you can count!" Bill said. "Sure, three's the limit, and we're too old to start breakin' game laws. Yeah, I guess that winds things up for this season. Be quite a while, probably, before we hunt any more pa'tridge."

They came out of the woods on the crest of a hill which overlooked the town, and Bill sat down on a stone wall to think. If he went South he would have to contrive some way to get the money, and there wasn't a thing except a few odds and ends left to sell. Just a few worthless tools—and the gun. It would be tough, letting the gun go, but there didn't seem to be any other way. He'd go down to the hardware store and see if Sam Tate would give him forty dollars for it.

Pumping out the three shells, he dropped them in the pocket with the other three that were left. "That's figgerin' pretty close," he said, drily. "Endin' forty years of huntin', with only six shells left over. I'll bet Mr. Burgess couldn't reckon much closer than that." He eased the old shooting coat across his shoulders and started down the hill toward town.

A nice, lazy, friendly little town, Bill thought, as he came from Elm into Main. The only folks who weren't really friendly were the bank people. Still, you couldn't blame them too much. It was business.

He could see the bank now, a block away, with three men just getting out of a big car in front of it. Businessmen, he'd bet, taking in those two bags of money. It must be a great feeling to be rich like that. Money couldn't mean much to them, the way the chauffeur was wasting gas. Even from that distance he could hear the engine, turning over fast, as though it were anxious to be off.

A pair of laced, knee-boots, in a window caught his eye, and he paused to look at them. They'd be nice to wear down South, but the price was eighteen dollars.

He started on again, then paused as a new thought seized him. It wouldn't do any hurt to step into the bank for a minute and see if Mr. Burgess had changed his mind about giving him a little more time. He shifted the gun to the other arm and stepped down off the curb.

Bill never knew when the driver stepped out of the car. The first unusual thing which caught his attention was the angry *zing-g* of a hornet passing uncomfortably close to his ear, and the instant crash of shattered plate glass behind him.

Zing-g-g! The hornet buzzed again, closer this time, and Bill did what any sane man would have done. A parked car stood less than ten feet away, and he made a flying leap to get behind it. He moved fast, but not quite fast enough, for the gun crashed again, his right leg jerked from beneath him, and he went head-first into the sheltering protection of the car, with the pointer at his heels.

Half stunned by the impact, he clung to a fender and tried to think. Someone had deliberately shot him, and for a moment he could not understand why. Then he knew.

"The bank! They're robbin' the bank!"

Old Bill had a hearty respect for the business end of an automatic pistol, but greater than his fear was an inborn hatred of the pariahs who preyed upon society over a leveled gun-barrel. They weren't men, but a bunch of white-livered rats, so afraid for their own skins that they would unhesitatingly shoot innocent bystanders. Bill was peeved and he had reason to be. When he tried to move the leg it dragged uselessly behind him. Who did the guy think he was, shooting at folks that way?

Although he had gone down hard, Bill had instinctively shielded his gun. Now he flipped the action open, dropped a shell into the receiver, slammed it shut and fed two more loads into the magazine.

Twisting about, he pulled himself erect with the aid of the fender. A swift glance over the car top showed him one of the robbers running from the bank, a leather bag in one hand and a pistol in the other. Stooping, Bill made a one-legged crow hop that carried him to the front of the car. Pushing the pump out ahead of him, he stood up.

Close by the open door of the getaway machine, the driver shifted his aim and looked along the sights. This time he intended to end it, but he waited a split second too long. When he was keyed up to it, Old Bill could kill a grouse as it flew through a ten-foot opening, and a shot like this was mere child's play. Without waiting to bring the gun to his shoulder he took a snap shot at the hand which held the pistol. He knew, even as he pulled the trigger, that he had nothing more worry about from that quarter. Sliding the action open and shut, he swung on the running man.

Holding low, he cut the fellow's legs from under him, and felt a grim satisfaction in seeing the unprotected face skid along the rough cement. Then the bank doors swung wide again as the two remaining men raced through them.

POW! Once again the gun roared and a robber stumbled and went down, but as Bill went after the fourth man he remembered that the gun was empty. A hundred times in the woods he had been caught thus, and experience had lent speed to his fingers. His right hand flashed to his pocket, came out with a shell, flipped it into the open receiver, while his left hand guided the gun outward and upward as he slammed the action home.

There was need for haste, for in that brief moment of time the fleeing survivor had leaped to the driver's seat. With throttle wide open, the car leaped away, but Bill grinned and went after his last bird. He had the two-foot square of an open window to shoot at, and he centered it. The echoes had not ceased drumming across the street when there came a tremendous crash, the top of a steel light pole careened wildly, while from it a frosted reflector came hurtling down.

"That stopped him," Bill said, and wiped a hand across his eyes, but it failed to improve his vision. Things began to blur and grow dark. For the first time in his life Bill was feeling faint. He tried to make it back to the curb, but the distance was too great, and he went down in a heap.

Years later he heard someone ask plaintively, "How can I? Do you want to see me get an arm bitten off?" He opened his eyes and saw, dimly, that the pointer was standing over him and growling menacingly.

"It's all right, boy," Bill said. "They're friends—I guess."

He was lying on a hospital bed that evening, gritting his teeth at the pain, but happy because they had told him the leg would heal and leave him without a limp, when a nurse came into the room. "Here's someone to see you," she said, and Bill looked across the room to see Mr. Burgess standing in the doorway.

"Hello," Bill said. "Come in." Then, as the nurse turned to go out he stopped her. "I hate to bother you," he said, "but there's a bunch of keys in my pants that I wish you'd get. Mr. Burgess wants 'em."

Mr. Burgess flushed and looked uncomfortable and cleared his throat a few times, but he did not speak until the nurse had returned with the keys, and when Bill passed them to him he took them.

"All right, Bill," he said. "Thank you. I'll drive out in the morning and arrange to take things over. It is my recollection that the buildings need rather extensive repairs, and I suppose that I should attend to that first. So take it easy, Bill. When you get so that you can hobble around you will have a home of which anyone would be proud. Yes, and you'll have a tidy nest egg in the bank, too. I don't know yet just how many rewards are coming to you, but they will be enough."

It was a pleasant dream, Bill thought. Too bad he had to wake up and spoil it. But the pain in his leg was no dream, and when he lowered his hand over the edge of the bed his fingers found a silken ear that was real, too.

"Gosh, Mr. Burgess!" he said. "That kinda changes things. Me and the dog were sort of plannin' a trip South this winter, but—well, I guess home will be a pretty good place for us, after all."

CHAPTER 6

Ghost Grouse

It is queer how events will roll along logically for months on end, and then all at once something will happen for which there is no explanation. Take those rifled slugs, for instance. Gene gave me five of them last fall to try out. I took them home and dropped them in the right-hand pocket of my shooting coat amongst a handful of woodcock loads.

The next day we were in an alder run looking for timberdoodles, and as I broke the gun and started to load it, I remembered the slugs. Unfortunately it has never been necessary for me to use rifled slugs in order to miss woodcock, so it seemed wise to sort them out and put them in the game pocket where there would be no possibility of using them by mistake. Bringing out a handful, I looked at them one by one, and after I had examined them all I repeated the performance. There was not even one slug among them.

I long since learned that it is easy for me to be mistaken, but I distinctly remembered dropping them in that pocket. I knew that it was not impossible to lose a shell or two while rolling under a wire fence or struggling up from a headlong plunge into a brush pile, but the odds against losing them all was at least a hundred to one. Pocket by pocket, I searched the coat, but they were gone. It bothered me. I knew it was senseless to ask my wife about them, but I plucked up my courage and did so. Her answer was what I knew it would be. She had enough to do without hiding my shotgun shells. So there the matter rested. The slugs were gone, but I did not know where.

Then, one day a month later, after the woodcock were gone

and we were hunting grouse, I shoved my hand down into a bunch of shells in that selfsame pocket and brought up two of those telltale, green-jacketed slugs. I looked at them for a moment and then investigated. They were there, every last one of them, in the very pocket where I had placed them a month previously, yet I had used the coat several times each week during the intervening period, and on several occasions I had drained that pocket to less than five shells. I have never learned where the slugs were during that time. I cannot even guess how they got out of the coat, or how they got back again, but I know they did both of those things.

Then there was that day in Desolation Cover. Gene christened it that years ago and the name is an apt one. A settlement was started there when New England was young, but although it lay in the fertile foothills, and stretched upward in a long, rolling slope which faced the south, ill fortune dogged the pioneers who cleared it. Some said an Indian curse had been put upon the land, while others thought an updraft of air brought a pestilence from the marshes that rimmed the distant lake. But whatever the cause, the effect was readily apparent.

Cattle wasted away and died mysteriously in the lush green pastures, while sheep succumbed in their first week on the land. Although the rank growth of all wild vegetation attested the fertility of the soil, yet hardly one cultivated thing would thrive. Corn sprang up sturdy and strong, yet soon yellowed and withered away, and even the hardiest barley and wheat would mildew.

Death stalked abroad in the land, and on each farm a rounded knoll soon bore its complement of granite grave stones. But the pioneers were made of stern stuff, and they hung on for nearly a century, hoping that the evil thing which lay upon the land would depart, but at last it wore them down. With their morale shattered, they one by one relinquished their holdings, giving them back to the wilderness to claim again for its own.

Strangely, although most other things nurtured by the hand of man ultimately withered and decayed, the apple trees—when once they had reverted to the wild state—flourished as I have seldom seen them do elsewhere. Immune to the winter frosts, and the snows which drift deeply around them each year, they continue to grow sturdy and strong, and each autumn the ground beneath them is covered with their yellow fruit. Deer come there in late fall to feast on the frost ripened delicacies, and in October, after the blackberries are gone, grouse trek up from the lowlands to fatten on the spicy apples and find safe haven o' nights in the thick covers of young pines which are inexorably claiming the land once more.

Whether grouse are on their periodic decline or increase, I know of few covers in New England which offer a hunter a better opportunity to burn a bit of powder, and Gene and I have made a practice of looking it over several times each season. Aside from the evidence that man had once cultivated the land, and the dreary desolation of the place, there had never been an incident to mark it from any of fifty other covers we knew. And then one day——

We had worked up through an alder run without flushing a bird, but on emerging from it we came to another of those rounded knolls on which a house had once stood. To the left of the old cellar hole and towering over a few, scattered, seedling pines, several thrifty apples trees grew. As the setter swung toward them he slowed suddenly, took a few cautious steps and froze in a solid point.

"Here's the first one," I said. "Probably under one of those apple trees. Go around to the other side and I'll drive her out to you."

Gene made a wide detour that carried him well around the trees, then worked in a trifle so that the bird lay between us, as we like to have them do. No matter which direction it might choose for its flight, it was probable that one of us would have a fair chance at it.

"Okay," Gene said, and I saw him hitch his sleeves up at the wrists and swing his gun free. "Let her come." I went in behind the dog.

"WHIR-R-R-R!" A grouse got up from beneath the trees and went hammering out, low down, on a course which would take it past Gene at a distance of less than twenty yards, and it is on cross shots like this that Gene really shines. Usually the birds who win their way past him in such a set-up are Luck's own children.

His gun cracked spitefully and I watched to see the bird somersault in the air, but not a single feather drifted from her. It is true that Gene, like all wing shots, misses birds, but if one is near enough and still in the clear, woe betide it when he goes after it a second time. I would not have given a thin dime for the bird's chance of survival when the gun cracked again, but it went serenely upon its way, unruffled and unharmed. I heard Gene make a remark which would never get past an editor—and then another grouse came out in the exact groove made by the first one.

I wish to point out that Gene does not get easily rattled. He has hunted grouse for years and knows most of the tricks. When the bird started he was in the act of stuffing another pair of shells in his pump gun, but he knew that only one was required to kill a ruffed grouse. Dropping the shells he held in his hand, he went after the bird, and he was doubly dangerous because of his previous misses. But in the open, within twenty yards of him, the bird turned its head to look disdainfully at him with its bright, beady eye, and he missed it cleanly.

I do not know what Gene said that time, for almost immediately two more birds came boiling out from the same place. The first one of the pair also went toward Gene, but the other one came up at a sharp angle, banked abruptly and came back, high and clear above the trees, within easy gunshot of me.

I'll frankly admit that I miss a lot of grouse, through careless shooting and accepting all the hard chances offered to me, but I do not often miss those who fly past me as that one did. However, I missed that one and, to make matters worse, I missed her again with the left barrel, while at the other side of the knoll Gene was pumping shot after shot at his bird.

When the tumult died I walked over to where he was standing. There was an incredulous and bewildered look in his eyes.

"That's a queer thing." He said it mildly, without a single qualifying adjective, which is an unusual thing for him to do in moments of stress. "I was holding on those birds."

I had not thought of it until that moment, but now I remembered that when I pulled trigger on mine I was aware of that pleasing, anticipatory thrill that a wing-shot feels when he is sure he is holding correctly. Something was screwy here. Even though I had been mistaken, there was still Gene to be considered, for he had long since passed the stage where he missed grouse in wholesale quantities.

"It might be defective shells," I suggested, weakly, but he scoffed at the idea.

"They were from the same box I used yesterday," he said, "and yours are a different gauge. It couldn't happen to both of us."

"No," I admitted. "It couldn't. But never mind. We slipped up on this chance for a cleanup, but let's forget it and get going. There are other birds in this cover."

I was a true prophet. In a corner where two stone walls met at a right angle, in a tangle of blackberry vines and over a rigid point, we put up two grouse simultaneously. Again Gene had worked around them, and again they broke so that each of us had a well nigh perfect shot, but we missed them as before.

"What's the matter here?" Gene asked, as we came together again. "Are we jinxed, or what has happened to us?"

I was beginning to wonder, for once more I had been confident that I was holding right. "Maybe old Chief Makosis has put the Indian sign on us," I suggested, banteringly, but Gene took it seriously.

"Things have happened here that have never been explained," he said, soberly. "Did you ever notice how many gravestones there are around here? They didn't use all the rocks in their stone walls."

"What has that to do with killing grouse?" I asked him. "We never had any difficulty here before."

"We're having it now, and there's something mighty queer about it," he said. "I was holding the gun on those birds. That's one thing I know."

I'll not attempt to explain what followed, for I frankly admit that I do not know. I hope no one will misunderstand me, for I have but little faith in the mystic and the occult. Somewhere there is a logical explanation for the things which we attribute to the supernatural, but it is not always easy to find them. Then, too, there is in every man an inherited something that goes back beyond cold logic: a thing which has come down to us from the time when men believe that the universe was governed by malevolent spirits who lurked behind each tree and stone, awaiting their chance to seize a luckless mortal and bear him off into the fearsome unknown. Thus it is that when something unusual occurs to disrupt the even routine of one's life, the primal instincts are prone to reassert themselves.

But that was no reason why the dog should go haywire. Until then, he had matter-of-factly tended to his job of finding grouse, and aside from a slightly contemptuous look when we failed to connect, he was unaffected by our mental letdown.

Now, as we went ahead, he acted differently. He had always been a bold going dog, sure in his knowledge of the birdy places, and just the least bit resentful of restraint; but all at once the intense eagerness which characterized his every movement seemed to be lacking, and he looked back at us more frequently than was his usual custom. I was aware of a growing conviction that he was somehow concerned about our safety.

We were, as I have said, on high land, and our wanderings had carried us more or less through beautifully wooded country, but as we emerged from it and came to a barren crest I saw that the grasses were stunted and lifeless, and although the summit commanded a view of much of the surrounding area, I remember thinking that I had never seen another place so lonesome or desolate.

It was Gene who called my attention to the sky. When we had entered the cover, the sun had been shining, but now we saw that the rounded vault above us had become overcast with a haze that cloaked the world in a peculiar, coppery light. Some weird quality about it made our surroundings seem unnatural, while the woods in the distance looked grim and foreboding, and among them the white branches of a few scattered canoe birches were tinged a spectral gray.

Below us, the lake was hidden in mist, while from the marshy land surrounding it a greenish, miasmal fog lifted and spread slowly in the suddenly dying wind, then billowed and rolled, and began creeping up the slope toward us.

Gene looked at it for a moment, then turned and looked at me. "This is a hell of a place to hunt birds," he said. "Let's get out of here."

From far away in the west, beyond the faintly outlined mountains, came a distant rumbling which was unmistakably thunder, and I could see that the light was fading more and more each moment. "There's something coming," I said. "A hurricane or tornado or thunder storm. All right, let's go."

It may have been because the car was a mile away, or perhaps it was because our course lay uphill, but my panting breath told me that we were hurrying, and I didn't like it. It looked too much as though we were running away. "Now wait a minute," I said. "Is there anything here that you are afraid of?"

"Who? Me?"

"Yes, you," I said. "Why are you hurrying?"

"Was I? I didn't realize it." He turned and faced me. "I know one thing, though. This has been a mighty queer business from first to last. Oh, oh! There's a point."

Framed in the edge of one of the numerous openings, the dog had jacked into a statuesque point, and the hunting instinct in us made us forget the events of the past two hours. Separating, we went ahead, our guns ready, waiting for a bird to take wing.

We came up to the dog and were taking another forward step, when the air was filled with sudden clamor, and from the ferns and stunted grasses before us, at least a half dozen grouse got up simultaneously and went sailing away toward the thicker cover.

Years of hunting have caused me to swing automatically toward the sound of rising grouse, and I did so then, but as I lined up the gun on one of the flock something stayed my finger from pulling the trigger. I knew they were grouse, but in that eerie light they resembled none that I had ever seen before, for each was tinged with that pallid, sickening copper hue.

My hesitation was only momentary, but any hesitation is too much when one is shooting at grouse. Recovering, I swung on another bird, but I knew that it was now too far away, and I lowered the gun.

As the reverberations of those startled wings died away, a great silence closed in around me, and I knew it was caused by the fact that Gene's gun had, like mine, remained unfired.

"What's the matter over there?" I asked him. "Why didn't you shoot?"

He came slowly toward me, and there was a troubled perplexity in his face. "I don't know," he said. "They looked queer, somehow."

It thundered again, a long, low, ominous rumble that began and ended nowhere, and yet possessed a power which seemed to make the earth tremble beneath our feet. We looked at each other without speaking, then, by mutual assent, we tucked our guns beneath our arms and went on.

A hundred yards ahead, near a thin fringe of cover, the dog pointed once more. I did not know how Gene felt about it but, for my part, I had had enough of the sort of foolishness we had indulged in. I knew I could kill grouse if they were in the clear and within range, even if old Chief Makosis was jiggling my elbow, and I proposed to prove it. I started ahead, and Gene swung into step beside me. Then we stopped, and stared at the dog.

Like all his points, this one was tense enough, but instead of straining eagerly forward he had the appearance of shrinking slightly backward, as though he had been suddenly confronted by an unexpected and fearsome thing. Even while we stood there staring at him I saw the hair rise along his spine and neck, and then he did a thing which I have never seen him do, either before or since. He took a nervous, cringing, backward step. Then he turned, tucked his tail between his legs, came galloping back to us, faced again toward the wood and growled menacingly deep within his throat.

For one brief instant Gene and I looked into each other's eyes. Then, actuated by a common impulse, we slipped the safeties off our guns and started forward, with the dog slinking furtively along behind us.

The wood, when we came to it, proved to be no more than a shallow fringe of trees which skirted another of the numerous openings. It was not dense enough for grouse shelter—but we were not looking for grouse. To this day I do not know what we expected to find, but certainly it was not grouse.

With every sense alert, and with our fingers tense upon the triggers, we pushed into the tangle, but in the hushed silence before the storm there was no sound or movement. Together we emerged from the trees, and there in the opening before us was another of those tiny, rock-walled enclosures, and within it a rough and irregular slab marked the resting place of another victim of the inhospitable and desolate land. We stared at it for a moment and once more looked questioningly into each other's eyes. Then, still without speaking, we turned away and went on to the waiting car.

There's an aftermath to the story, of course, but instead of explaining the former events it makes them even more baffling. We went back there a few days later. The dog's work could not have been excelled by a national champion, Gene achieved a snappy double and a brush-busting single while I was accumulating two, and we did it with the expenditure of only five shells.

CHAPTER 7

Toby Was a Bird Dog

Not all infant prodigies make good when called upon to face the stern realities of life. On the other hand, some backward, cross-gallused urchin of whom the most optimistic teachers despair, goes out and astonishes the world by setting a river afire.

Consider George and Steve, two youths of my acquaintance. At the age of nine, George could compute five columns of figures simultaneously, and play around with cube roots and logarithms as happily as though they were a family of puppies. Steve, a year older, had little more than a shaky conviction that two and two made four. Now, at the age of fifty, George draws a meager pittance from a kindly welfare agency. Steve died a few years ago, but when that unpleasant event occurred he was president of one of the country's leading manufacturing concerns, and was a member of the board of directors of more than thirty associated firms. He was a trifle slow in developing, but he had what it takes to make good.

There are bird dogs like that. At the age of six months, *Lady,* my setter bitch, was hunting like a whirlwind. A month or two later she was pointing grouse, and doing a pretty fair job on those birds who permitted her to make her tumultuous approach upon them. Bill's *Toby,* a two-year-old pointer, still plodded sedately along with us, sniffing at woodchuck holes and fox burrows, listening with a slightly bored expression to the thunder of rising birds, and looking at us questioningly from time to time, as though he were asking us what it was all about.

It was annoying. We had wasted many precious days the previous fall in trying to arouse his hunting instinct, and before the season closed I had decided that he would never become a bird dog. The beginning of the second season confirmed my belief, and I told Bill something to that effect.

"You are wasting your time," I said. "If it's a pet that you want, you can't beat him. But if you want a grouse dog you'll have to dig down into your jeans and buy another."

Taking scent from the air.

Bill took it more kindly than do most men whose dogs one ventures to criticize. "As he stands now, he ain't worth a nickel," he agreed, "but he'll come along in time. His father and mother were grouse dogs. He's got the stuff in him somewhere."

"If he has, it is buried so deep that it will never get to the surface," I said, in my omnipotent wisdom. "He is two years old and he has never pointed a bird. Life is too short to fool with that kind."

He took it without malice, but his is a stubborn mind. "I'm

going to string along with him for a while longer," he declared. "I'm going to give him a fair trial."

Such was the beginning of the career of one of the three greatest grouse dogs I have known. His metamorphosis from nothing is one of several wonders I have witnessed in my time, and should be worth the telling.

It was late October. The leaves were well off the alders and birches, and ruffed grouse were seeking the higher ground. Leaving the car, Bill and I swung into a stand of second growth beeches which crowned a long ridge. On either side it was flanked by water worn gullies that were choked with junipers, and on the higher slopes thrifty young pines grew.

It was an ideal place for grouse. Beechnuts lay everywhere beneath the trees, furnishing an ample and well liked food supply. Two hundred yards away, the pines furnished the safest of night protection, and in their daily journeyings back and forth the birds could pass beneath the junipers and be safe from attack by any raider from the skies.

We had not travelled far before *Lady* began to make game. As we started to follow her, Bill, as was his custom, called to the pointer in an endeavor to get him in on scent before the bird took wing. Once again he was unsuccessful. A rabbit trail had caught the dog's interest and he had wandered off on it. I could see him down below us at the edge of the junipers, looking back at us as though to say, "If you fellows feel that you must hunt, why, for goodness sake, don't you come down here where there is something which is at least a little bit interesting?"

Ahead of me, through the trees, I could see *Lady* go flashing about in an ecstacy of excitement. That was her greatest fault. The scent of grouse did something to her feet, and made them carry her too fast at the crucial moment, but nevertheless I could not help comparing her favorably with her stolid companion. She was in there, casting about in an effort to locate the source of the scent which was in her nostrils, while *Toby* was a hundred

yards away, sniffing at a second-hand rabbit track. The bitch
was worth a hundred such as he.

Lady did not nail the bird, but blundered upon it as she all
too often did. It came out in a roaring rush that carried it past
me at a distance of nearly forty yards. The distance was too far
for a clean kill, but something prompted me to break my usual
practice of restraint on such chances and take a snap shot at it.
As the report rang out I saw a wing-tip flip upward: the bird
rocked in its flight and then went slithering down in a long slant
which would land it well out in the junipers. Watching closely,
to mark the spot where it must inevitably crash, I saw the
pointer lift his head and turn about to face the bird.

The grouse saw the movement, for the dog was almost directly
in its path of flight. It tried desperately to change its course, but
the dangling wing-tip was too great a handicap, and it came
down within thirty feet of the watching dog.

That, I decided, was one bird which was going to be hard to
find, for not only did the junipers extend all the way to the pine
woods, but in addition it offered a thousand secure hiding places
within itself. I do not seriously object to missing a grouse, or a
dozen of them, but I do dislike leaving a crippled bird to suffer.
With my eyes still on the spot where this one struck, I waited for
Bill and *Lady* to come over and help me with the search.

Lady's enthusiasm knew no bounds. She threw caution to the
four winds and went over the junipers like a thoroughbred at-
tacking a high hurdle. With head held high, and ears flopping,
she bounced through them, paying no attention to my commands concerning the point where she should begin her search,
and relying on her energy more than upon the nose which nature had given her. We knew that only by blind chance would
she be successful, so we began a systematic quest, keeping only
a few feet apart, and lifting the prickly branches so that we could
peer beneath them.

From time to time, as I straightened up, I could see *Toby*

looking at us, and at last something in the earnestness of his gaze attracted my attention. I am firmly convinced that there is an unexplained sixth sense which dogs possess that enables them to fathom many of the emotions which stir within human minds. Although I had not suspected it until that time, *Toby* not only had that sense but he also had an extra-sensory perception. *Lady's* excitement interested him not at all. She could jump her fool head off for all he cared, but the seriousness with which we attacked our problem seemed to have him worried. He watched us for another moment or two, then plowed in behind Bill and began sniffing in and out among the pungent branches.

"Atta boy," Bill said. "Find 'em."

Toby looked inquiringly up at him and a light began to dawn in his eyes. I could almost imagine him asking: "What is it, Boss? What are you looking for? If it's that rabbit, he's been gone for hours."

"Find 'em," Bill repeated. "Find dead bird."

"Eh?" the eyes said. "Bird? You don't happen to mean that half-grown hen that flopped down here a minute ago, do you?"

"Go find 'em," Bill ordered again. "Fetch."

Quite deliberately *Toby* turned and walked out of the junipers. Then, still unhurriedly, he went for fifty feet along their edge, then began working his way into them. They were higher than his back, and only occasionally could we catch a flash of white to mark his progress. Then that ceased, and from the spot where he had just stood I saw the white spike of his tail emerge from the tangle and stand aloft with ramrod straightness.

"It looks like he's nailed her," Bill said, quietly, as though he had been doing it all his life.

It was exactly as he had said. Without fuss or bother, the pointer had gone to the spot where the bird had hidden beneath a mass of gnarled roots, and had nailed it there like a veteran. We dug it out and made quite a fuss over the dog, but he was as modest as a Quaker maiden.

"Everybody to their fancy," he might have said. "Now if I were to get all steamed up over anything, I'd choose rabbits for mine. But if you say it is to be grouse, why, that goes."

We called *Lady* back—she was cruising the pine woods by that time—and started on. Once more the little fly-away took the lead, running with throttle wide open merely for the joy of being alive, but after a time she struck scent.

There is an intoxicating odor, a heady effluvium, emanating from grouse which casts a spell on most dogs. Many a one will tiptoe up to a woodcock or quail with all the dignity of an undertaker going about his macabre tasks, but with the first whiff of the more exotic odor he will become as light headed as a bobby-soxer at a rock'n roll contest. It was beginning to dawn on me that *Lady* was one of that type. Irresponsible enough at best, she now cast aside all caution and began a series of looping spirals that had neither objective nor purpose. Round and round she went, and the faster she travelled the more she seemed to believe that even greater haste was called for.

We stood and watched her, Bill and *Toby* and I, and each of us was thinking his own thoughts. Mine were of a defensive nature. I was trying to convince myself that high spirits were a necessary requisite in any hunting dog; that *Lady* was young; that in the course of time she would find out what her nose was for and be a credit to my judgment in selecting her.

Bill didn't say anything, but I knew him well enough to read the thoughts which were running through his mind. Schooled in stern New England thrift, he was thinking that here was a tremendous amount of power going to waste: power that might be far better employed in running a sewing machine or churn, or some other profitable endeavor. He was thinking, too, and quite rightly, that nose and brains are the two fundamental requirements in all hunting dogs, but he was too polite to voice his conviction that *Lady* had neither.

What *Toby's* thoughts were, I'll not venture to say, but I'll swear that he had plenty of them. He looked at Bill, and then he watched *Lady* do another series of her mad gyrations. After that, he strolled down to a shallow depression whose rim *Lady* had skirted twice, and straightened out in a solid and matter-of-fact point.

Bill killed the bird, the first reward for his months of endeavor, but his natural reticence is such that he made no comment on the work of either dog. My own reaction was a natural one. I had been prejudiced against *Toby* for his lack of interest, and I could not yet attribute his two finds to anything but sheer luck. It merely happened that way. There was no other logical explanation.

We killed five grouse that day. Two over *Lady's* errors, and the other three over *Toby's* stanch points. His procedure was the same on each occasion. *Lady* winded game, and while she was flying around in an effort to locate it, he roaded in and nailed it. He displayed little of the fire that I like to see in a grouse dog, but I noticed one thing that was to his credit. When he went in, his course was as straight as an arrow's flight. He knew exactly where the bird lay.

The next morning, when I drove into Bill's yard, he came out with his coat, his gun and his lunch, but no dog.

"Where's *Toby?*" I asked.

He said, apologetically, "I figgered it would be better for both of them if we work them separate for a while. Take mine tomorrow, if you don't mind."

We followed that plan for a few days while I was getting my education. Then one morning, when it was *Lady's* turn, I drove into the yard without her.

"Where's *Lady?*" He echoed my query of the previous morning.

"At home—where she belongs," I answered, for about the only virtue I claim for myself is the ability to swallow my medicine without making too wry a face. "She'd never be a bird dog if she lived a hundred years.

There followed several years to which I look back with nothing but pleasure. I have hunted over quite a respectable number of dogs, but only two of them were in *Toby's* class, and neither of them was quite like him. He liked grouse hunting, but only when he smelled a cottontail would he really glow with the inner fire that one commonly associates with bird dogs. On countless occasions I have seen that electric ripple run along his body when his nose told him that a bunny was crouching under a near-by brush heap, and every instinct within him cried for him to flash into a point on the creature, but he never did so. Instead, after a hesitating moment, he would circle the retreat warily, like a reformed drunkard who crosses the street rather than pass the doors of a saloon. Then, with temptation safely behind him, he would continue with the business of finding grouse.

Toby was not what one might truthfully call a good woodcock dog, although his fault was not like that of other superlative grouse dogs I have known. Theirs was the too careful approach, the result of their schooling on the infinitely more highly strung ruffed grouse. His failure lay in his lack of enthusiasm for the little russet chaps, but he somehow sensed that we liked them and he pointed them dutifully and, on occasion, even when the more alluring scent of grouse was in his nostrils.

I recall one day when, going in high headed after a running bird, he paused and swung his head around at an acute angle to indicate to us a woodcock which lay within six feet of him. So eloquent was the gesture that we each understood it. Bill bagged the woodcock when it bounced up before him, and I downed the grouse a moment later when it took wing. Then we waited with interest to see what the dog would do. He retrieved the grouse first, with tail awag and eyes merry, then went dutifully in and brought the woodcock out.

As I recall the days that I spent in the woods with him a score of incidents arise unbidden in my mind, but three of them are most vivid in my memory.

It was another crisp October when all the grouse in the county should have been out on the hillsides, but the grouse population was spotty that year. It was disappointing, for I was trying a new gun, an auto-loader, and my brief experience with it had led me to believe that what I needed most was about two weeks of old fashioned shooting to mold myself to the idiosyncrasies of its cumbersome breech and bulging fore-end.

Toby was in his fourth year, and was a grouse dog of whom any hunter might be proud, but he had never yet looked upon me with any degree of confidence. Bill and I were passable shots, and there was little difference in our percentage of misses, but *Toby* would not believe it. He believed that the destruction of any bird in the air was caused solely by the magic of his omni-potent master.

The only times when he showed unseemly haste was when I downed a bird while Bill was some distance away. He would dart in then, grab it and go galloping away to lay it in the hand of the boss; and if I chanced to get to it first he would look at me while I stowed it away, and in his eyes I could read a great and unspeakable contempt. "Why, you low-down, miserable sneak-thief," they seemed to say. "Stealing a bird that belongs to *him!*" Then he would shun me for an hour or more, staying on Bill's side of the cover, and looking accusingly at me when-ever I drifted over that way for a moment.

The first of the three incidents occurred one day when we had worked through a fair sized swamp and, somewhere in the outer fringe of bushes, had lost sight of *Toby*. We stood there a few minutes, waiting for him to come back, but when he failed to return we knew he was on game.

"Where did you see him last?" Bill asked, and when I told

him it was off to our left, he moved away in that direction, while I continued straight ahead to the higher ground.

Toby was there, in a tangle of birches and blackberry vines, locked up on a bird. Without too much confidence in myself, but with the clumsy weapon pushed out before me ready for instant action, I went in and paused close behind the dog. Instantly, some thirty feet ahead, a grouse hammered up toward the tops of the birches. New gun or old, I couldn't miss a shot like that, and I tumbled the bird back to earth.

Although I had shot almost directly over the dog's back, he did not flinch or move a muscle. Then, as I looked at him, he swung his head an inch to the right, and stood there without a quiver.

"Another one?" I asked him, and a second bird flushed, beating sharply upward as the first one had done.

Again I connected, and again the dog swung his nose another inch to the right. A third grouse came out, exactly like the others, and I tumbled that one back with the rest. Still, *Toby*

Something's going to happen soon.

had not moved an inch, but now he took two infinitely cautious steps and froze once more. This thing, I thought, might well become habit forming, and if it proved to be so, I was willing to become an addict. Then the fourth and last grouse came out to meet its fate.

It was, and still is, the only time in my life when I ever killed four grouse without moving from my tracks, but *Toby* seemingly was more impressed by the feat than I. I won my spurs that day in his estimation. He went in after a bird, picked it up, stopped to think for a moment, then came out and laid it carefully down before me. Without a word of advice from me, he went in after another, trotted back and deposited it beside the first. Then he brought the third and added it to the rapidly growing pile. He stopped then, looked up at me for a moment, then considered the offering he had laid at my feet. I don't pretend to know how I knew of what he was thinking, but I did, or I at least guessed right. He found the fourth bird, picked it up, and without even one backward glance at me, started off in search of Bill. The score, in his opinion, was a trifle one-sided.

The second incident concerns a day when *Toby* had company. There is a justifiable rivalry between men who own bird dogs, and I am glad that it is so, for it tends to improve the breeds. Furthermore, I would not give a whoop and holler for the man who wouldn't back his own dog if it chanced to be a good one, although I believe it should be done in a gentlemanly manner. In my code it is all right for a man to throw out some pretty broad hints that his dog is tops in finding and handling birds, but I think he should use a bit of discretion in making derogatory remarks about the rest, especially before he has proved his right to do so by open competition.

There was, in a neighboring town, a gentleman who did not subscribe to this belief, and eventually his remarks reached Bill's ears. The result, as I have said, was that *Toby* had a bracemate in the woods one day, while two twenty-dollar bills lay in the cash till of the local hardware store awaiting the winner.

The boasting gentleman had a good dog, and he promptly proved his worth by promptly outdistancing the moderate going *Toby* and smashing into a spectacular find. Ten minutes later he duplicated the feat, and then went on to do it a third time.

Then *Toby* woke up. His nose had always been superlative, but he had been accustomed to adapt his pace to our more leisurely ones. Now he began to realize that if he found birds he would have to use his legs also, and he promptly stretched out in his casts, always refraining from heading the other dog when they chanced to choose a similar course, but always crowding him to an ever faster pace.

It was not long before it had its effect. Going at top speed, *Toby,* warned by his superior nose, would slide into an abrupt point, while the stranger, with tongue hanging, would go on to bump the bird. Then, when he had him thoroughly demoralized, *Toby* really opened up. He had the competitive spirit, and what he showed us that day was something to remember always. It was too one sided to be called a race, for after the first few minutes the other dog never had a chance. *Toby* outshone him as a mercury light outshines a candle, and the boaster acknowledged the fact before the day was half done.

"That's enough," he said, for he was built of the right stuff after all. "I thought I owned a world beater, but I didn't realize how much territory that covered."

The third incident concerns Bill rather than *Toby,* for *Toby* was beyond caring. I missed the merry drumming of his feet on the frozen ground when I drove into the yard that morning, and the memory of all the happy days we had spent together came poignantly back to haunt me.

Bill was standing by the corner of the barn, resting his hands on the high board fence, and staring out across the frost browned slope where *Toby* used to course in his youthful and irresponsible days. He turned at my hail and came out to rest a forearm along the open window of the car.

"Come on, Bill," I said. "Get the gun and let's go."

He did not answer, but stared down at the gravel underfoot.

"Come on," I urged again. "It's tough, but we have to learn to forget them. It will do you good to get out into the woods."

"I know it," he said, and I saw his lip quiver. "I know it, but —tomorrow I'll be all right, but I'd rather not go today—if you don't mind."

I understood. *Toby* wasn't my dog, but he had won a pretty big place in my heart. I decided I would rather wait until tomorrow, too.

CHAPTER 8

You Have to Know Them

It had rained during the night, a real old New England gully-washer, but early morning brought clearing skies and a gentle west wind. A morning like that in mid-October is made especially for grouse hunters; so I did not bother to phone Gene. Instead, I drove over to his home and found him sitting on his doorstep, his coat and gun resting across his knees, and a pointer cuddled under each arm. Many years of hunting together has made us psychic in a small way. He knew that I would drive over. I knew that he would be ready to go. What need of a telephone?

A half hour later we were driving over a nightmarish back road, for we had long since learned that super highways and ruffed grouse were not compatible. Halfway through one axle-dragging stretch, we came to an extensive swamp. From the slopes surrounding it the rain had converged until the swamp was nearly awash.

Bumping and splashing through the deep ruts, we at last rounded a corner and came to abruptly rising ground. Through the mud-spattered windshield I caught a glimpse of a sumac-clad knoll and, behind it, a growth of scrubby young pines. Suddenly Gene said "Whoa!"

I stabbed the brake so hard that a dog catapulted into the front seat. "What did you see?" I demanded. "A water-buffalo?"

He grinned. "Let's look this place over. It ought to be good for a bird or two."

The knoll looked birdy, I thought, as I got out of the car. Its blackberry vines and sumac meant that the sort of food which grouse like could be found there. The sun was shining down warmly, too, on the sidehill, but we had already passed a half dozen spots which looked equally good. Without much enthusiasm I snapped the gun together and dropped in a couple of hulls.

Old *Rap* and the pup had been doing a limbering-up exercise down the road, but now they came tearing back. Twenty feet from the car the old dog swerved and leaped the ditch like a thoroughbred taking a hurdle. Watching, I actually saw him stiffen in mid-air. He struck square-footed and stayed there, with head and tail high, the magic of hot grouse scent making him youthful and dynamic once more. In the center of the road the pup stopped sharply to honor his old man's point. Gene was coolly feeding shells into his pump. Taking a few dry shots at random trees and posts to limber our arms and shoulders, we went in.

Whir-r-r-r! A grouse rose a scant three feet from the ground and went darting in and out among the sumacs. I missed her cleanly with the first barrel but caught her with the other, and like echoes to my shots Gene's pump spat viciously twice. In the hush that followed I heard the spasmodic drumming of wings upon the rain-soaked leaves.

"Did you get yours?" Gene asked.

"Yeah."

"All down in this alley, too," he said. "I busted a pair of 'em."

The dogs retrieved the birds and then gave the knoll a quick once-over without striking scent. We were on our way again in less than ten minutes.

"How did you know the birds were there?" I asked him.

He gave me a pitying glance. "Anybody ought to know that," he said. "Birds are still using the swamps, but they aren't using them today unless they have grown web feet. They had to be some place, and this was the likeliest looking spot."

I believe that incident summarizes the secret of successful grouse hunting. I care not what a man's ability may be with a shot-gun. If he doesn't know his birds, a good grouse hunter will wipe his eye five days out of every six they spend afield together. He will do it because he will secure shots for himself at a ratio of two to one, and he will secure them so naturally and so easily that the other will never suspect he is a victim of anything but his abominable luck.

Any normal man who will shoot a weekly round at skeet during the summer can learn the fundamentals of wing shooting, and can acquire a skill sufficient to kill a fair percentage of his good shots at birds within the range to which he has become accustomed; but if he wishes to hold his own with a seasoned grouse hunter he must serve a long apprenticeship in the woods. He will find innumerable angles there that can never be duplicated on a skeet range.

In the big woods in Quebec, in the Maritime Provinces and also in northern Maine and New Hampshire I have seen numerous grouse that might have been killed with not too long a stick, but it is an unusual experience to find a dumb one in any locality that is even occasionally hunted. To all species of wildlife, man is the great educator, and a town-reared grouse wins his sheepskin with a celerity which would astonish even a present-day college president. He is equipped with a hearing device which is second to none, his protective coloration is well-nigh perfect, he is as crafty a strategist as any bird that flies but, despite all that, he may be hunted successfully if one will observe a few fundamental principles.

In his distinctive classic, A SPORTSMAN'S SCRAPBOOK, the late Dr. John C. Phillips remarked: "It has always seemed to me that the foundation of success in this kind of hunting is based on learning how to walk, and particularly how to walk on rough ground so as to never lose balance." I am convinced that the good doctor had something there. Probably more grouse are missed because of faulty footwork than one would naturally suppose. If a man is off balance, or is trying to regain a balance

already lost when a bird flushes before him, he is doubly handi-
capped, for nothing is so conducive to good shooting as properly
placed feet and a gun properly mounted to the shoulder.

The secret of walking correctly lies, of course, in charting
one's course as he drives his car, looking at a point which is still
several steps ahead, and retaining a visual image of the hazards
which lie between.

Also there is an ever-recurring problem of maintaining adequate vision ahead. It is a glorified and perpetual game of check-
ers in which the hunter must constantly ask himself, "If I move
there, which way will the bird go?" The most poignant and
frequently used lament is, "If I had just gone around the other
side of that tree I'd have had a perfect shot at her."

For sheer skill and daring in hurtling at full speed through
dense cover, no other upland bird deserves to be mentioned in
the same breath with the ruffed grouse. At full speed he will
flash in and out among the tree trunks and a miscellany of
smaller stuff, and seldom brush a wing tip; yet I know of no
other bird, except it be a pheasant, who so thoroughly dislikes
to fly.

That trait, in the days of the market hunters, caused the un-
timely deaths of untold thousands of grouse. Men who knew his
habits and habitats set rows of pencil sized stakes across swamps
and runways which the birds customarily travelled, leaving at
varying intervals openings sufficiently large for the bird to crowd
through. The stakes were never more than two feet high, yet
instead of flying over the obstruction the grouse would work
along its length until he came to one of the openings. Whistling
cheerfully because he had found a way to avoid using his wings,
he would thrust his head through the opening—and a spring-
pole powered noose would jerk him abruptly into the air. It had
been reported that catches of a dozen or more have been taken
from one line in a single day.

He will wander from his roosting place in the early morning, then loiter and peck his way to some exposed hillside for a dust bath and a few hours of idle sunning. Then, as the afternoon wanes, he will retrace his steps, feeding ever more briskly as the shadows lengthen, until he has reached his chosen roosting place for the night.

If unmolested he will follow that routine for days and, with the exception of his ascent and descent from his perch, will never once take wing. He knows the same reluctance to fly when he hears an approaching hunter, unless he happens to be in an exposed position or one in which he fancies he is cornered, when he will usually take wing at once. His preference, however, if he is in cover dense enough to hide his movements, is to steal quietly away from the area which he thinks lies within the line of the hunter's approach, but before he moves he wants to definitely know just where the danger lies.

He is jittery, for experience has taught him that he may be in for a few unpleasant moments, but instinct tells him that his coloration makes him practically invisible as long as he stays on the ground. He is considering the possibility of flight, but he will not ordinarily take wing if he knows definitely where you are, and feels that you have not yet crossed the line which he has mentally designated as the last inch of safety for him. For that reason I have come to believe that a system may be evolved which will frequently fool him.

My shooting companion and I have hunted together for twenty-five years and naturally we have worked out a plan which serves us well—sometimes. When he is working the dog I lay my course parallel to his, and approximately the outer limit of the dog's casts to left or right. I try as best I can to watch the dog in order to know if he is winding game. If he works momentarily in front of me I know that I can relax, wipe the sweat from my brow, and the leaves from the neck-band of my shirt, and inwardly glow with the expectation of what lies just beyond.

Presently I am aware of my companion's murmuring voice.

It is not loud and—for the dog's benefit—it is not the least bit excited. Just a flat and lifeless monotone, but it thrills me like nothing else in the world.

"Over here on point," the voice says, "but kinda swung around your way a bit. High headed. Bird lays up in front of you, I should judge. Cut around a little more to your right. More yet. There, that ought to be about right. No, the dog is turning his head a bit to the left now. Bird is swinging over this way, I guess. Pick your spot and I'll put her out to you."

Turning sharply, he goes quickly ahead, his gun poised for instant action. He is watching his footwork, too, for he knows the penalty of being caught off balance when a bird rises and, as best he can, he chooses a path that will give him an unobstructed view of the restricted area in which he believes the bird has momentarily paused.

If everything has worked according to plan—and it sometimes does—he continues his advance until he believes the bird lies directly between us. Then he turns abruptly toward it. Theoretically we have now presented ourselves with a perfect setup. We are no more than forty yards apart, the cover is fairly open, and any bird that gets up between us is a dead pigeon—still theoretically.

The grouse is in a tough spot, unless it keeps its wits. It knows it is surrounded, or at least it did know, but we try to make it forget for one fatal moment. For a half minute I have not moved a muscle, while my companion has not only tramped steadily toward me but has also kept up that ceaseless flow of chatter. Perhaps the bird will forget that I am standing there. I am keyed to high C, yet as motionless as the pointing dog. I grin as I listen, for there is now a hint of exultation in my partner's voice.

"Fooled us last week, didn't you, old biddy? Well, it looks like it was the other way round today. How are you going to get out of this mess, eh? Well, come on. Make a stab at it anyway. Scat! Shoo! Get the heck out of there."

If the cover is sufficiently open he may make a sudden jump forward, landing in shooting position again, but with a startling thump. Or he may cease his chatter, take two or three catlike steps ahead and then pause quietly. Either method will usually

A grouse dog must be high headed.

bring the bird into instant, roaring life, but more and more often of late a canny old bird will show a marked reluctance to commit suicide in that manner. There is a chance that, with head turned and one beady eye glancing warily back, it will steal quietly ahead for a few yards, then thunder out and corkscrew its way through the thickets, flying so close to the ground that the ferns will sway in the winds of his passing. Hard shots, these, calling for a swing that is fast enough to carry the muzzle past the bird, a conscious effort to hold low—and a fervent prayer. Occasionally the latter is answered. Then, oh boy! What a glorious feeling.

I have learned that a novice can go through a cover which contains birds and not find them, but an old-timer develops an instinct which tells him where the birds will be at a certain time, and he will invariably locate most of them. Neither animals or birds lead a haphazard existence. The pattern of their daily lives may be quite accurately charted, and if any man will put in the time to study his favorite quarry he will learn many things which should work to his advantage.

From their roosting places grouse move in the early morning hours to their feeding grounds. They eat lightly throughout the day, but about two hours before dusk they begin to feed in real earnest. Gradually their crops grow round and hard as they distend with the gorged food, until they become almost as round and cylindrical as a baseball. I have taken many more grouse than I ever expect to kill again, yet never, with the exception of a few times in late fall when the first snowstorm of the season was beginning to leaden the morning skies, have I taken one that had a full crop before the late hours of the afternoon. It is nature's way of stoking the fires with sufficient fuel to last through the long night hours.

Knowing then the feeding habits of grouse, and remembering their characteristic disinclination to fly unless disturbed, one should be able to tell quite accurately where the birds in any cover will be at various times throughout the day. In the morning they are quite likely to be along the edges of thick, coniferous growths. If flushed they will almost invariably fly toward this shelter. Therefore when two men are hunting together one should choose a route which will keep him between the dog and the wood. He will then be in the proper place to go to the dog

if he secures a point, and will also be in the best possible position to intercept the wary bird that takes wing immediately at
the sound of the dog's approach.

Later in the morning the birds spread out in search for food
and, under certain conditions, will travel long distances in order
to feed upon some extra choice delicacy. I have known them to
work down a long slope of a pine crested ridge, cross the valley
floor (a boggy morass that formed an almost impenetrable barrier to humans), ascend the steep slope of the opposite side, and
there gorge themselves upon the meaty white-oak acorns which
could be found only in that one restricted area.

I spent many priceless hours that fall on both ridges, watching
them come and go, and so unconcerned about my reclining and
motionless figure that once one of them stepped on my foot as
he hurried past! The crest of those two ridges were at least a
half mile apart, but I never saw a grouse fly either to or from
the feeding ground. It is only on rare occasions, however, that
the birds will wander so far from the old homestead. Two or
three hundred yards is usually the limit they care to venture
from their sheltering evergreens.

An apple tree in even the scantiest cover will usually draw
grouse from a considerable distance, not only in the fall but also
in mid-winter when they feed upon the succulent and vitamin
packed buds. During the fall any fruit laden tree is almost certain to have a bird either in it or underneath it. One wise old
dog with whom we hunted for several seasons used to point automatically when he came within smelling distance of one. I suppose he had figured that the law of averages would make him
right more often than wrong, and it usually worked out that
way. Incidentally, grouse are connoisseurs in their taste for apples, and frequently feed exclusively on the fruit from one tree
in a group of several.

I know of no other one thing which helps more in finding
grouse than the practice of dissecting the crops of the daily bag.

What one learns thus is truly "inside information" which cannot be disputed. If I find that the birds are feeding largely on thorn plums or acorns or apples or dried blueberries, I can then make a mental survey of the covers I know which abound in whatever food the autopsy discloses, and hunt them at once. It usually pays big dividends.

There is a lot of both kinds of luck in hunting any species of game, and I am grateful for all of the right sort which comes my way; but my greatest thrill comes when I know that I have outsmarted a wary old bird who has fooled me on other occasions. If the knowledge I have gained through long association with a cover leads me to believe that a pair of birds may be found at some particular spot in it, and if my judgment tells me they will fly in a certain direction when flushed, and if I arrange to be there at the moment of their crossing, then the fact that I may miss them both does not detract from the success of my day.

I have matched my cunning against the superlative cunning of a ruffed grouse, and I have succeeded in outwitting him. I know there will be other grouse in other covers, and if I am wise enough to remember my schooling I will be in the right place to intercept some of them as they rocket back toward the shelter of the pines.

CHAPTER 9

You Still Have to Point Them

Offhand I don't know how many years I have hunted with Old Fred, and I am not going to reckon back and find out. I tried it once and it scared me. But I bought a setter pup from him once, and went back the next fall to show him what a mistake he had made in selling him, and so we drifted into a yearly week-end get-together which has lasted ever since. He knows his dogs and his birds and, in addition, he is one grand guy. Therefore it was with keen anticipation that I drove into his yard one crisp October morning last fall.

Opening the car door, I let *Jack* out to walk stiff-legged around Fred's *Bob,* in the delightfully informal way they have of getting acquainted again after a year's separation. Then I went into the house, knowing that they would be good friends again after the make-believe rumpus was over.

Fred was ready, or nearly so, which tells its own story of the efficiency of a sixty-year-old who operates his own farm and a small dairy, yet manages to get away by eight o'clock in the morning on most of the good days during the season. I drank a cup of Mrs. Fred's coffee while he was gathering up a few loose ends, and then we went out to where the two dogs waited happily together beside the car.

"Where are we going?" I asked, as I backed the car into the road.

"I dunno," he said. "The Black Brook cover, I guess. I found two good flocks in there yesterday."

"Good flocks?"

"Yeah," he said. "Good in this day and age. Must have put up seventeen or eighteen birds."

"As many as that? How many did you leave?"

He lowered the window, knocked the dottle from his pipe, then stowed it away in his pocket. "About seventeen or eighteen," he said.

"Were they wild?" I asked.

"No," he said. "That's me you're thinking about. I was—and still am."

Something in his tone made me look at him sharply, for he had not been his usual jolly self that morning. I wondered if he were sick, but decided that if that was the case I wouldn't mind catching the disease, for he looked to be good for at least forty more years.

"Well," I consoled him, "it takes a bit of time to get in shape after a gun has been sitting in a corner for ten months." But even as I was saying it I wondered if his age might be beginning to tell. After all, a man's eyesight doesn't last forever, and keen eyes are one thing he certainly needs in bird hunting.

"Yes," he agreed. "Yes, I guess it takes time all right," and then he fell to talking of other things until we reached the cover.

I could remember when this was as fine a bit of grouse country as ever lay outdoors, that mile-long-strip of flatland, for it was bordered on either side by gently rising slopes of birch, while a deep, sluggish brook ran through it. Now the alders were rotting at their bases and the land had gone sour. Still, there was plenty of feed on the hillsides, and if Bill said the place contained grouse I knew we would find them there. I let the dogs out of the car and slipped into my shooting coat.

"Ho-hum," said Fred and, opening his gun case, he drew out a new and sparkling pump, twisted it together and worked the action experimentally.

"Ah-ha!" I said. "A new one, eh?"

"Yeah." He slid three shells into the magazine and pumped

one into the barrel. "Yeah, I'm playin' a slide trombone now."

I knew then the reason for his glumness and why there were still seventeen or eighteen birds left in the cover, but it seemed wise not to discuss it. If he had any shooting problems he was fully capable of working them out for himself, and would prefer to solve them alone.

In their first wild dash for cover the dogs bumped a lone woodcock at the very edge of the run. *Jack* swung around to quarter the ground carefully lest he pass up another, but *Bob* paused and watched the bird's flight and then went in and nailed it promptly when it fluttered down to earth fifty yards away.

"Your bird," I said, as we went in together. "I'll kick her out for you."

It came up to the tops of the alders with the characteristic, whistling spring that makes the flight seem faster than it really is, hovered there for an instant while the shot charge sped harmlessly past, and then went flitting lightly away.

Fred said, "Six," rather grimly, and stuffed another shell into the magazine.

"What do you mean, six?" I asked.

"Somehow me and this corn-sheller can't seem to get organized," he said. "I've been out of step with it from the first and it's growin' worse all the time. That's my sixth straight miss."

"You'll get used to it in a few days," I told him, but I wondered if he would. He had been shooting the same old double ever since we first met, and it had become as much a part of him as the hands which guided it. I knew that he was capable of riding out a bird with the pump, or with any gun, and killing a fair percentage of them, but he was an instinctive shooter, and I wondered if, at his age, he could master a weapon so different from the one to which he had become so accustomed.

Two hundred yards farther ahead *Jack*, while finishing a cast which took him to the brook, wheeled sharply around and came roading out toward higher ground, while *Bob* slowed his smooth stride and came angling across toward the same spot. Directly past Fred they went, a pair of workmen who knew what they were doing, and froze solidly at the very edge of the alders.

A fellow learns something about his dog after he has followed him as many seasons as I have followed *Jack,* and by the intensity of his point and his high and rigid flag, I knew that a grouse was lying close before him. The setup was perfect, for the ground was particularly open at that spot. The alder run lay at our right, but ahead and to the left there was no hindering thing. Just a few small bushes and clumps of juniper bush. Fred slipped the pump from beneath his arm, mounted it experimentally, then stepped in behind the rigid dogs.

Three grouse came out from behind a juniper and started across the clearing, waist high and in perfect fan formation. If I have seen Fred take a pair under similar circumstances I have seen him do so a dozen times, and I would have taken a moderate bet that right then he would make it a baker's dozen; but although he went to it with all his oldtime smoothness it was no dice. He emptied the pump and did not ruffle a feather.

"Nine," he said, mechanically, and stared bewilderedly at the spot where the birds had disappeared.

There isn't much that a fellow can say at a time like that, so I laughed it off with the old platitude about the best of men having their off days, but he only shook his head and muttered something under his breath.

Ranging ahead, *Jack* winded one of the trio, roaded it out into the alders and pinned it there. It lay beautifully, but when I put it up it corkscrewed away through the tangle instead of breaking into the clear. I took a quick, instinctive snapshot at it, but luck was with me and I cut it down.

"Nice work," Fred said heartily, when I came out, but somehow I did not feel elated. In fact, I found myself rather dreading the remainder of the day and the two that followed it. Killing birds is but a small part of the pleasure the game should hold, and this week-end promised to be about as cheerful as one spent in a morgue.

One of the remaining singles had treed and went rocketing away after we had passed it, but the dogs found the other one well up on the hillside. As they so often do after a long flight, this one lay like a woodcock, and got out from almost beneath Fred's feet as he went in.

Armed with his old double, he could have taken one good look at the bird, then closed his eyes and either killed it or else given it the closest call of its life, but now he missed it cleanly twice before it had fully straightened out in its flight, and then flubbed the perfect chance by not working the action far enough. I think I could have taken the bird then but I would not do it. The poor fellow was sufficiently demoralized already and I did not want to make matters worse. But he seemed to derive a grim sort of pleasure from it, for he said "Eleven," and managed a ghastly sort of grin as we went on.

Halfway through the cover, the sidehill curves in a long crescent, and at one place thrusts an arm out into the swamp almost to the brook. Often I have seen the dogs begin to tighten up long before they came within possible scenting range of the place, for memory told them that they would certainly find birds there. Now I saw *Jack* stick his nose in the air and go angling off toward it.

"That's where I found one of the flocks," Fred told me. "It looks like they were back there again."

The dogs were there before us when we came up, stretched out gloriously and trembling in the abundance of scent. We edged away from them on either side in an effort to get the birds between us if possible, then went boldly in.

There is a tremendous thrill in the take-off of even one grouse, but when a half dozen or so explode simultaneously from a nearby spot, one really gets his money's worth. It had been a long time since I had walked into such a layout, for we had the birds between us, and they went up to the tops of the alders like so many woodcock. Feathers drifted away in the breeze as I cut the props from under the first one at a distance of less than twenty yards, and the left barrel caught another at only slightly greater range.

A stone's throw away I could hear Fred's pump blasting away like a company of marines, and after *Jack* and I had retrieved our birds I went over to see how he had fared. He had thrown his hat on the ground and was stamping round and round it.

"I've learned to count to ten when I'm mad," he said, "and this time I've counted to fifteen, and I'm damned if I ain't got a good mind to say somethin'."

"Don't mind me," I said. "I'm fireproof. Cuss as much as you like."

"It ain't the gun that's got my goat," he said. "If I was thirty years old instead of sixty I could learn to shoot it in a couple of days. The thing I'm mad about is the circumstances that made me buy it. I didn't want to. Cripes! I paid a hundred and forty dollars for the old double, and it's as good as it was the day I brought it home. It'll still cut a hair when you close it in the breech."

"Then why did you change?" I asked.

"Dang it, I had to." he said. "The old girl's got Damascus barrels, and you know what this new speed stuff is doin' to 'em. I kinda want to keep my fingers a while longer."

"If I were you, I would stick to the old gun and old-time ammunition," I advised him.

"That's fine," he replied tartly. "That's just lovely. You tell me where to buy it. Order 'em special? Every doggone dealer in the state has fallen for a line of bunk, and you can't buy nothin' but high-speed stuff."

"I guess you are right," I admitted, "but don't call it bunk.

These new loads certainly pack a wallop and reach right out after 'em. There's no bunk about that."

"Is that so?" he argued heatedly. "Look! My old man killed forty-two straight ducks with an old muzzle loader and black powder."

"That's a poor argument," I reminded him. "Conditions were a lot different in those days."

"How were they different? The ducks were the same, and so were the pa'tridge. Yes, by golly, and so were the men. They learned to shoot with what they had, and they killed game with it too. My dad couldn't have killed those ducks any deader with dynamite."

"No, but he might have killed some which were out of range of his old Queen's arm."

"Well, maybe," he admitted, "but I doubt it. Fifty yards is about the limit for a 12-gauge. Oh once in a while there's been somebody like Fred Kimble or Hansen Lambert who could stretch it out another ten yards or so, but ten yards less is the limit for the majority of folks. There's too many factors of wind and flight speed to be figgered when you go beyond it, and there always will be, no matter how much they speed up the loads."

I recalled some of my experiences in point and pass shooting, and was forced to agree with him. "But you will have to admit there is an advantage in higher velocity and a shorter shot string," I said.

"Advantage to who?" he enquired. "I can't see that it has been any advantage to me so far. If I have learned to kill a cross shot at any distance from ten yards up to forty, without lookin' at the gun or thinkin' about lead, I don't see how it's goin' to help me any if the charge gets there before I want it to. And as far as a short shot string is concerned, that's plain bunk. Man alive! When a bird moves across a long shot string, it makes up for any holes in the pattern. Anyway, with the old double I hit my birds with the center of the charge, and that means the middle of it, any way you figger it. They can't do any better'n that in Boston, whether the pattern is as flat as a barn door or strung out like a funeral procession."

Slowly but surely he was penning me in a corner, but I still tried to wriggle out. "We can't go back to the horse and buggy days," I said. "Science is making tremendous strides everywhere. If we old-timers can't keep pace with it, it's too bad, but that is no reason why we should try to stop the clock. We have to think of the younger generation."

"I am thinkin' of 'em," he protested. "I'm thinkin' that science ain't helpin' either the next generation or the game supply when it is tryin' to make weapons that will kill 'em both off any easier than it can be done now. And it ain't right to tell a youngster that he can kill birds at seventy-five or eighty yards with a shotgun. It's bad for him and bad for the birds, and eventually it's goin' to be bad for the feller who lied to him. Science! Bah! I see where they're tryin' to invent some kind of shot that'll dissolve in a duck's gizzard without poisonin' him. Heck! If they'd invent some that would dissolve in the air at forty-one yards they'd be doin' somethin' worth while."

"All right," I said. "you win. And now how about trying to find a few more birds for you to miss?"

He grinned without rancor. "Okay," he said, "but I get hot under the collar when I think about all the stuff I see in print. Accordin' to them advertisin' fellers, all there is to killin' game is to buy their brand of guns and shells. I wish I'd had 'em here this mornin'. They'd have learned that you still have to point the gun at 'em."

It has always been something of a mystery to me how a flock of grouse can scatter and manage to get cleanly away, especially if they are given a few minutes in which to perfect their plans. Follow a flushed single immediately and your dog will usually find it within two hundred yards. But scatter a flock and then try to pick them up one by one, and more often than not you will be disappointed. Seemingly they are more jittery, and will either run like turkeys or fly at the first suspicion of pursuit.

We found that the rule held true on that occasion. The dogs located three which had already got together, but they flushed before we got within gunshot of them. From somewhere up among the birches we heard another one go a minute later, but although we ranged back and forth for a half hour we could find no more.

"They needn't be afraid of me," Fred said, as we gave it up and started on. "I'll guarantee not to hurt 'em."

At the upper end of the run, where some young pines and maples were beginning to creep in, I saw *Bob* hesitate for a moment, then road ahead with his nose in the air as it picked up a distant scent. Fifty yards farther on he slid into a point that looked like business, and it looked even more like it when *Jack* went in and backed him promptly. As we came up, a bird flushed from behind a thick tangle, hammered into the tops of one of the pines and stayed there, while the dogs loosened up and went ahead. Then, as I have seen him do so often that it no longer surprises me, *Jack* stuck his nose almost straight up in the air and pointed again.

"She's treed, and *Jack's* got her," I said to Fred, who was working in from the other side.

"That's nailin' 'em. Get set and I'll try to drive her out to you."

It is the kind of shot that I do not like, especially when I have an audience, for with the force of gravity to help him, a grouse can zoom outward and downward and achieve top speed almost instantly. However, it was a bird, and it was lying—or standing, if you prefer accuracy—to a point. In justice to the dogs, someone had to take the shot, and Fred was very definitely not up to it today. I went around the clump of pines.

"All right," I said, when I came into the clear, and I heard him go in.

Presently there came the clamor of beating wings, an echoing report and a startled exclamation.

"Dog-gone!" he said. "I killed her deader than Julius Caesar."

He was holding the bird in his hand when I came back, and there was a look of incredulous surprise on his face. "She came out of the top of that tree like a hawk after a rabbit, and went down within four foot of the ground," he said. "Now wait a minute. There's somethin' here that needs to be figgered out."

"Go to it, Sherlock," I told him, for I knew that no one was more capable than he to solve a scatter-gun mystery.

"She was near enough so I didn't have to lead her," he went on, "so that's taken care of. This gun has the same drop and pitch as the old double, and the same length barrel, but the receiver makes it three inches longer. That would have a tendency to pull the muzzle down a bit, don't you think?"

"Perhaps so," I admitted.

"You're darned tootin' it would. Come on. Let's go find a bird."

We crossed the brook, worked through the alders to the outer edge and headed back toward the car, with the dogs cutting busily back and forth in front of us, working boldly and high headed as grouse dogs should do, yet ready to slow their pace the moment they winded game. Following along in the direction they had taken, we topped a low ridge and came upon them, heading back toward the lowland, and solid as granite.

There was no mistaking Fred's purpose as we went in, for he was bent upon redeeming himself, and twenty years seemed to have rolled from his shoulders in the last few minutes. I eased into an opening where I could have an unobstructed view, and watched interestedly as he came up to the dogs.

A grouse came out from the edge of the run and went away like a jet plane on a speed test flight, but good old Fred was organized at last, and he took her with his old-time snappy swing. His face was beaming when he came back.

"Never saw her at all," he boasted. "Just looked at a spot two foot over her back and let go. I've been holdin' under 'em."

It seemed that he had found the answer, and I was sure of it some ten minutes later when a bird that I had missed crossed in front of him, thirty-five yards away and going as only a thoroughly frightened grouse can go. He centered her so accurately that feathers snapped from her in a fleecy cloud which drifted idly away across the alder tops.

"It ain't goin' to be a bad little gun after all," he said, as he stowed the bird away and came back to where I was standing. "Got to learn to point it, same as you have to with any gun, but I guess maybe I'll get onto it after a while. Hm-m! Mighty nice day, ain't it, now that the sun has come out."

"It has been shining all morning," I informed him.

"Has it?" He seemed surprised. "It sure looked gloomy to me."

Once more the dogs were ranging joyously ahead, and once more we followed happily behind them. A crow cawed raucously in the distance, while down by the brook a white-throat warbled his silvery lay.

"That last bird was quite a long way out," Fred said at length. "Did you notice how I smacked her down? Darned if I don't believe these loads have got quite a wallop."

CHAPTER 10

You Can Hit 'Em

Ask any five shotgun toters in my neck of the woods if they can hit flying birds, and three of them will give you an unequivocal "No." The fourth will boast that he is having a poor day when he doesn't bag at least three doubles, thus certifying himself to be a charter member of the Ananias club. The fifth man, that quiet fellow with the restless eyes which notice each windblown leaf will, if you press him, admit that he kills a bird now and then, but misses far too many for his own peace of mind.

It has been my good fortune to hunt over quite a bit of territory. In the time it has taken me to do it I have met a lot of interesting people and made many dear friends. One of the best of them is also one of the best all-round wing shots I have ever known. On grouse, pheasants, woodcock, ducks or geese he is a cool, consistent performer who takes approximately fifty birds with each hundred shells he expends. I cite his case because I believe it remarkable in view of the fact that he was nearly thirty years old before he killed his first flying bird.

He had given the game a whirl for a couple of seasons, but had been forced to conclude he was not adapted to it. But a little urging and a little coaching, plus a couple of summers of trapshooting changed his way of thinking, and in only two more seasons I was paying strict attention to the laurel wreath which perched so precariously on my brow. In that short span of years the fellow had learned to shoot like nobody's business.

I have no reason to think he was particularly gifted. An analysis of his style convinces me he had no more than average ability,

126

but he had the wisdom with which to discover his mistakes, and the dogged determination to correct them.

Therein, I believe, lies the answer to a great many failures. When a man pulls trigger at a target without knowing whether he is shooting at it or merely in its general direction, it is not enough for him to vow that he will aim more accurately the next time. Pointing a shotgun at an inanimate object is not a difficult feat, and on most straight-away shots it is equally easy. The man who misses them consistently must find out the cause.

If it is overanxiety to possess the quarry, he must school himself to think and actually believe that it is merely a pound or so of good meat which, so far as vitamin content is concerned and at present prices, he could duplicate at any meat counter for the trifling sum of two dollars and ninety-eight cents. If it is the momentary paralysis which is the common affliction of most beginners when a bird flushes, he should be able in the course of time to discover the fault and train himself to overcome it.

I am convinced that the momentary stiffening of the muscles when a bird rises unexpectedly is not a handicap which is suffered by beginners alone. It frightens me when I think of the number of years which have elapsed since I killed my first grouse, but I know that there are times even now when that nervous reaction bothers me. There are times when it seems that the birds are getting the jump on me. They are the times when it seems imperative for me to hurry if I am to line up on the target while it is still within range. I cannot prevent its happening occasionally, but I have learned an effective remedy for it. When I say to myself, "Brother, at the next whir of wings, forget about looking for the bird, but swing your gun at the sound," then things revert to normal and usually stay there for a time.

A commonly accepted belief that grouse and pheasant are too fast for any shooter who is not especially endowed by the gods is entirely false. It has been estimated that a woodcock in high gear can do not much more than 20 m.p.h., that the top speed of grouse is approximately 30 m.p.h., while that of the pheasant is variously estimated at from 40 to 60 m.p.h., although it is my opinion that the first figure is more nearly accurate.

On the ruffed grouse, that speed works out at 44 yards in three seconds. In that space of time an average man should be able to empty a five-shot pump-gun. Or put it another way. A good sprinter can do 100 yards in 10 seconds. Starting from scratch with a ruffed grouse on a cinder path, he could cover his 100 yards and still have the bird in extreme shotgun range, or approximately 46 yards away.

From still another angle, show me the tyro who doubts his ability to stand beside a highway and consistently spatter the backs of the highly polished cars which pass him at 30 m.p.h. Or 40. Or 60. Why, after a little practice, if he could keep out of jail that long, he could almost do it with his eyes shut. "But," someone will say, "the automobile is a big target." So it is, but if one can center it he has done all that is necessary in order to kill flying birds.

I vividly recall one instance which may serve as another illustration of the amount of time required to center a rising bird. A grouse had flushed wild before my dog on a cut-over lot which gave me an unobstructed view for several hundred feet. The trees had been cleared to the very edge of a narrow country road, but on the other side a thick stand of young spruces grew. Watching the bird's flight, I saw it pitch down at what I believed to be the edge of the road.

Now here was a layout which seemed to demand some mighty fast gun work. If the bird lay where I thought it did, and if it flew directly toward the nearest cover, which it almost certainly would do, it had not more than thirty feet to go in order to win its coveted shelter. In other words, in less than one second it would be irrevocably out of sight.

With that in mind, I went in behind the dog who had now established a point, and the bird flushed directly toward the friendly barrier. I covered it with the gun and then waited for what seemed like an eternity while I let it go the last possible inch so that the charge might open into something more than a meat-grinder pattern, and then I squeezed the trigger. Sensing that a mighty short distance separated us, I took nine long steps and picked up the bird, and I could have stopped it in practically half that distance.

To a startled hunter it may seem that any game bird achieves its maximum speed instantly, but this is far from the truth, especially if the bird is beating up through heavy cover. In every case a certain amount of inertia must be overcome before the bird is in free flight. On more than one occasion I have seen a trigger-happy young novice pump two shots in the general direction of a rising bird before it had reached the tops of the ten-foot alders that it was trying to surmount.

More birds are lost through too hasty shooting than by any other cause, but it is also true that the one-eyed-sighting chap who rides out his birds will never become an accomplished wing shot. It happens many times that one is forced to wait until the target emerges into reasonably clear view, but the best shots I have known have all had a style which was similar in one respect. Some were naturally fast while others were slow, but they all went after their birds with a steady swing, and shot at the first instant the barrel moved into what they believed to be the proper alignment.

There is something mighty demoralizing about trying to realign a target, as any man who has ever flinched at a trap-shooting range will testify. If one is looking toward the future, and striving for better co-ordination of hand and brain, it is better to waste a charge on a poorly aimed shot, than to concentrate on correcting it. Disregard it and try to make the second attempt ring the bell.

Concentration on the business of the moment is a factor which should be stressed. I have never believed that the sound of the human voice was particularly terrifying to any species of upland game. Many a time I have said things to a close lying bird which would have caused any creature with an ounce of sporting blood in its veins to come out and fight, and it never had any visible effect. But when two people are engaged in a spirited conversation they are not in the best mental attitude to intercept the flight of a suddenly sprung bird.

I learned that fact early in life, and I learned it from my old friend Bill, the shooting mentor of my youth. He was old enough to be my father. He did, in fact, as I have related, take a fatherly interest in my shooting. He also tried—and I like to believe with some small measure of success—to teach me how to hunt.

I was a garrulous kid, and I know now that I must have got on his nerves from the start, but he stood it for a time. Then, one day when I was errupting with even greater vigor than usual, he stopped and eased himself down on a grassy bank. "Son," he said, "Talking is a serious business, and so is hunting, but they don't rightly mix. Sit down and we'll gab a while. After that, we'll go out and try to pick up a mess of birds." That advice was worth remembering. Hunting is a serious business, if one is hoping for a bird in the pot. When one is carrying on an entirely needless conversation, or merely thinking about last night's date, he is giving himself a bigger handicap than he can afford to take.

In learning to hit game there is no substitute for shooting at it. The era which produced the breech-loading gun also produced the greatest wing shots the world has ever known. It is probable that their records will never be equalled: certainly not in the amount of game killed, and almost equally certain in the percentage of hits made. At first blush, as the saying goes, it might seem logical to believe that trap and skeet shooters who have runs of several hundreds to their credit would be equally

deadly on birds: but fortunately for our feathered friends it is
not true.

The clay target game is good practice. In fact, if one can explore it from all its angles, it is the best available practice. It
teaches timing, lead, angle of flight and all the seemingly necessary functions of mind and body, but it still is not bird shooting.
It is a game in which the shooter becomes definitely grooved.
Despite the wide variety of angles thrown, there is still a marked
sameness in their pattern. The intial speed of the clay target is
its greatest velocity, which rapidly decelerates as it encounters
wind resistance, whereas the flight of the bird is the exact reverse.
The clay target rises from a pre-determined distance and soars
at a pre-determined angle. Shooting at a pre-determined pace,
the marksman breaks or misses them at a pre-determined distance. Interrupt that smooth sequence by even a minute degree,
and watch the shooter's score fall off until he has mastered the
new factor of corrected lead and timing.

The upland hunter of twentieth-century birds faces an entirely different problem, for in the course of the season he will
have targets presented to him from every known angle, and
from some hitherto unsuspected ones. In the woodcock he will
find a slippery customer who may vault to the tops of the alders
as though launched from a catapult, only to hang suspended
there for what seems like long seconds before it rights its body
to sideslip and drop earthward in a long, erratic slant. Or the
next one may corkscrew away through the thicket in a zigzag
pattern that would shake loose the feathers of a jack-snipe if he
tried to emulate it.

The ruffed grouse may swoop earthward from a tree limb
with the speed of a stooping falcon, or it may hammer up
through the interlacing branches as slowly as though it were
climbing a stepladder. The pheasant may go out of a cornfield
as though jet propelled, or it may knock the hat off your head
as it fans aloft from beneath your feet in a briar tangle. All

these, and a hundred other things, present problems which may be more or less duplicated by a good man with a hand trap, but nothing has ever been invented—with the possible exception of the electric chair—which will give a hunter such a devastating, nerve-paralyzing shock as the sudden thunder of frightened wings.

There is a lot of hocus-pocus foisted upon a gullible public in the matter of guns and ammunition, which is confusing, to say the least. Groping for some tangible thing which will improve his shooting, Joe Hopeful reads that if he will equip himself with a certain make of weapon and a particular brand of ammunition, he will be able to take his daily limit of game, even though he is wearing smoked glasses and has one hand tied behind his back.

Almost sold, he turns a page and finds the argument flatly refuted. Only gun No. 2 can achieve the results he hopes to obtain. Joe is now groping in a mental fog, but he still erroneously believes that if he can find the right weapon he will be all set. Poor Joe. Probably the old double that sits in the corner would serve him as well as any if he would take the time to familiarize himself with it.

I like good guns, but the truth of the matter is that any American-made weapon of average quality, with any make of fodder for it, is capable of doing far better work than it will ever do in the hands of the average marksman. I am not intimating that one should not give a lot of thought to the selection of a shotgun. If he is not of average build he should be doubly cautious and seek expert advice in obtaining the gun which meets his physical requirements: but in the end it its long familiarity with a tool which makes it seem the best of its kind, whether it is a scatter-gun, a handsaw or a hammer. The gun is seldom responsible for the misses. The fault lies with the chap who is looking down the barrel.

Despite all the high-pressure advertising there is no magic

ammunition. Unless one cares to tote one of the magnums, the effective range of any shotgun is still on the negative side of fifty yards, and because of the various factors of wind, flight speed and increased lead, it is doubtful if it will ever be extended many yards.

The secret of success in shooting is to shoot and shoot until the coordination of mind and muscle becomes instinctive. Pattern your gun with various sizes of shot, and use sheets of paper large enough to take the entire load. Fix in your mind the distances at which the patterns will surely be effective when properly held, and shoot at no game beyond that range. Shooting at greater ranges will result in a greater proportion of misses and a higher proportion of crippled and lost birds.

My observation leads me to believe that any man who has a firm determination to master the game can become a good wing-shot, although I am not at all sure I would recommend that he try it. Ordinarily it is a long and uphill road in which there are a lot of seemingly insurmountable objects. It may be that the chap who finds a full quota of happiness in wandering the woodland trails and settling for a mixed bag is the wise one after all.

But if the thunder of rising birds is a siren song which thrills him to his very toes, there's a heap of consolation in the fact that he can stop a lot of them if he'll run enough ammunition through the old blunderbuss.

CHAPTER 11

Dear Jimmy

Dear Mr. Spiller

I wonder if you will help me. I want to be a grouse hunter but am not having very good luck at it. I am almost fifteen years old. My dad is going to give me a dog and gun on my birthday—I think. I have told him it's what I want most. What breed of dog is best? What kind of gun do you use?

I'm crazy about bird hunting and baseball. I'm a pretty good pitcher but an awful poor shot. I've been out quite a lot this fall with a fellow who has a gun. I've used almost two boxes of shells but I haven't hit a bird yet. Do you think I can learn how?

Yours truly, Jimmy.

Dear Jimmy:

You have handed me a tough assignment. If I could teach grouse hunting in one easy lesson I wouldn't have to worry about my future. It's a shame that we live so far apart, for I'd like to have you with me for about five shooting seasons. You wouldn't be missing all of them at the end of that period, Jimmy.

You wonder if I will help you, and you ask if I think you can learn the game. The answer is yes to both questions. Wing shooting is something that any normal youngster can master if he really means business, and nothing gives me greater pleasure than to start one of them off on the right track.

Because it is the one prime essential and the only tool you'll need, we may as well start with your gun—and lest you have some false belief concerning guns, let's first of all get down to fundamentals. Some of the finest wing shots the world has ever produced lived in the days when breech-loaders were unknown.

It is true that there were men in those days who were master craftsmen. They could turn out guns that possessed both feel and balance, but scientific methods today are producing weapons that are far superior. Strength, ease of handling, pattern—all these have been improved, as have the speed and power of loads. It is obvious then that when a grouse sails away unharmed, and you disgustedly toss away your two empty shells, the fault does not lie in the gun but in your manner of pointing it.

You'll half believe this now, Jimmy, but the time will come when you will seriously doubt it. You'll spend all sorts of money trying to find a weapon that will automatically point itself, but you are due for a big disappointment. Such guns will never be built; and if they were, you and I would never use them. We'll never be pot hunters, Jimmy. We will win or lose strictly on our own merits.

Because you are nearly fifteen years old you will soon be able to handle a gun of standard dimensions. Choose the gauge and the make that you like best. The style doesn't matter much. A double, a pump or an over-and-under, whichever type you prefer is the one to buy. If it is a twin tube affair, have the first barrel bored an improved cylinder and the other one a modified choke. If it is a single barrel, I would recommend a modified choke. You could, of course, if you plan to do a bit of duck hunting on the side, have an adjustable choke installed on the single barrel gun, but it will be of no benefit to you in the brush. Ninety per cent of the birds at which you shoot will be well within range of your improved cylinder pattern. Incidentally, tell your dad that a gun of fairly good quality is the cheapest in the end. If you take care of it properly it will last a lifetime.

When you throw the gun to your shoulder and cuddle your cheek naturally down upon the comb, your line of vision should be just slightly above the breech. In other words you should just barely see the whole length of rib above the barrels. If it

fits you like that you will be able to see all of your bird as you
pull the trigger.

I'd advise you to learn to shoot instinctively, with both eyes
open, and never once consciously try to line up your gun by
sighting over it, or to try to ride out a bird. Shooting thus, you'll
never be the world's best marksman—but you'll not be its poorest one either. About half the shots you get will be of the instantaneous variety that must be taken in a split second or not at all.

You'll miss most of them at first, Jimmy, and you'll heap
blasphemy on me, on your gun and on the world in general,
but there'll come a time when you'll stop one that had only
ten feet to go to reach cover. When that day comes I'll get my
reward, for as you store the bird away you'll look at the dog and
say, in a sort of happy wonder, "By golly, the old boy was right
after all."

The thing I'm trying to impress upon you is that you must
make the gun a part of yourself. You say you are a pretty fair
baseball pitcher. Well, you didn't learn it in one Saturday afternoon. No, you have been at it for years, and I'll wager that the
side of the old barn you used as a backstop has many a shattered
board that it received in your struggle for speed and control.
Those two things are the chief essentials, whether you are
facing a batter or swinging on a ruffed grouse. It requires a lot
of practice, but if you try long enough and burn enough powder,
the time will eventually come when you can slap the gun to
your shoulder, and the charge will smack home right where you
are looking.

There's another thing in favor of that type of shooting. You'll
find this hard to believe, but the time will come when your
eyes will be less keen than they are now. You'll notice that there
are three small converging lines in your forehead, and you'll
move the floor lamp over by your chair when you read, but if
you have learned to shoot as I hope you will, that handicap
will not make much difference to you. Daylight or dusk, in the

woods or on the marshes, if you can see 'em at all you can still hit 'em.

There are a few other things you should learn about guns. They are made to kill things with, and they are as democratic in their choice of victims as anything you will ever meet. They are always loaded, and when they accidentally discharge they always point in the one direction where they can do the most damage. I wish that I might impress this on your mind, but I know you will not take it seriously—at least not yet. Your hair will have to stand on end once or twice first, like mine used to do when I had hair.

Always carry your gun with the safety on, even when you are going in ahead of your dog to put up a bird. Don't laugh at me, for it is entirely practical. I've hunted that way for a lot more years than you have yet seen, and I assure you that when you have acquired the habit it will not retard your shooting by the millionth part of a second. You'll slap the gun to your shoulder and, by some miracle that you will never quite understand, the safety will be off.

I'm insisting on this for two reasons, Jimmy. The first is from the standpoint of safety. Guns, as I have told you, are dangerous weapons, but those of a reliable make positively will not explode a cartridge while the safety is engaged. The other reason is that many, many times while your dog is quartering back and forth before you, you will see him flash into a point, and hear a grouse take wing at the same instant. If you have schooled yourself as I suggest, you'll be ready when it breaks into view: otherwise you'll just stand there foolishly, staring after the departing bird, while your clumsy hands fumble all over the gun in their search for that elusive button.

So much for the tools of your trade, Jimmy, and now about dogs. Next to your gun, a good dog is a prime essential. You ask what breed is best. There is no best breed. There are only superlative animals of each breed. Your choice will be limited to pointers and setters, or perhaps a Brittany spaniel. All the spaniels are bird dogs, but only the Brittany will point. The others flush their game, and that is something that you will want to do yourself. You'll learn to love that moment when you pause to figure just where the bird is lying, and you will delight in trying to outguess it. For that reason you will need a dog that stands its birds.

Don't get the erroneous belief, though, that a dog can smooth out all your shooting problems, or assure your coming in with the limit each night. It is quite to the contrary. You can kill more birds without a dog than you can with a poor one, and the difference with a reasonably good one is not so great as you may suppose. But killing birds isn't everything. You doubt that, do you? Well, let's get back to baseball a moment and see if I can make you understand.

With the bases loaded, two out, and the count three and two on the batter, you get a whale of a kick out of breaking your fast one across the outside corner for a third strike, but I'll wager that if that was all there was to the game you wouldn't stick to it long. It is the smooth working of the whole team, and all the unexpected and unforseen problems that have to be instantly solved, that makes the game the fascinating thing it is. Similarly, you and your dog and gun will compose a team of which you will be both captain and manager, and your standing in the league will depend largely upon just how good a manager you are.

You will not know very much about training your first dog, Jimmy, and there's little I can tell you that will help. You will probably buy a lot of books on the subject and learn them all by heart. They will give you a general idea of what the experts demand in their dogs, but a thousand books cannot give you the one practical thing you need most. That thing is experience.

So it's a pretty safe bet you will spoil your first dog. You'll love him from the moment when you first gather him into your arms. You will never permit anyone else to feed him. You will doctor him and worry over him when he is sick. You will feed him from the table. You will take him to bed with you. You will even teach him parlor tricks, which is supposed to be the depths of degredation—or should I say dogredation—in bird dog circles.

You'll let him take charge and run the team, and lead you around wherever he chooses to go. He will break almost every rule in the game, but you will understand him better than you will understand another dog. He will find birds for you, and after a while you will be killing your share of them, and he'll bring them in to you, his head held high and his tail wagging joyously.

He will grow old all too soon, Jimmy, and some morning when you call him you will fail to hear the happy patter of his feet as he comes to greet you. You will cry when you bury him and, for a time, you will be more lonesome than you ever were before in all your life. Then you will have other dogs, a lot of other dogs, but some night as you sit alone before the fire that has burned low on the hearth, your memory will hark back to those first joyous years, and you will say to yourself, "I wish I had old *Jack* back again. He was the best dog I ever owned." Listen carefully for a moment then, Jimmy. I think you will hear the old glad thump of his tail from where he sits waiting for you upon a golden stair.

You will not make so many mistakes with your second dog, for you will be twenty-five years old then. You will have stopped your experimenting with guns, and will settle down with one you are beginning to swear by rather than at. Hunting will have assumed a still more serious aspect, and you will demand nothing short of perfection in your dogs. You will wear out barrels and barrels of shoes and check cords and spike collars and tempers in teaching him to quarter. You'll insist that he hunt close in thick cover and spread himself all over the landscape in open country. You'll teach him to retrieve promptly and tenderly from both land and water, and you will skin him alive if he ever breaks shot.

That's all mighty fine, Jimmy—I guess. But there's another factor you may not have reckoned with. Your shooting will have grown better in those ten years. It will have improved so much that you will be crumpling a lot of birds that you couldn't have pulled trigger on ten years ago. This means that you are going to have your share of cripples, especially broken winged birds.

With the possible exception of a pheasant, there is no bird cleverer on the ground than a broken winged ruffed grouse. He can and will run like a quarter horse. He can disappear within a brush pile or juniper patch as utterly and completely as a smoke wraith dissolves in mid air. He will crawl into a hole that is only half the size of his body and he will stay there for hours while your dog dashes helplessly back and forth around his hiding place. It is a peculiar thing, Jimmy, but you will find that it is true.

If your dog is good he is a body scent dog. When he winds a bird he sticks his nose in the air and goes to it, even though it is fifty yards away. The warm, rich scent of the bird's body is to the dog what a radio beam is to a flyer. They both go in on the strongest part of the beam. But a broken winged bird, crouching tense and motionless beneath a juniper bush is a different proposition. A spaniel or a hound would pick up the trail and run the bird down, but your dog will not do that, unless he is an uncommon individual indeed. He is dependent on that radio station which now is emitting only the weakest of signals, and he is well nigh helpless.

If he had committed the unpardonable sin of breaking shot, he would have had the bird shortly after it hit the ground, but in doing so he might—and mind I say *might*—have bumped another bird that you also might have brought down with a broken wing in another juniper jungle. So you will have to choose whether you will occasionally come home with the memory of a hard hit bird that was left to die a lingering death, or with the satisfaction of knowing that your dog didn't even wink an eyelash until you ordered him on.

You will hear a lot about stanchness but I hope you don't gather a false impression concerning the word's meaning. About the worst fault a dog can have is to freeze into an immovable statue when it first scents game. Translated into English it means, "I think there's a bird around here someplace, boss."

It is a thing that you strongly suspected; otherwise you wouldn't have bothered to look the cover over, and no matter how flattering it may be to have the dog corroborate your judgment, it doesn't help you a bit. What he should say, and say with absolute certainty, is "Boss, oh boss! There's a bird under this bush just ahead of me." When he makes a definite statement like that you'll have something to work on.

You mustn't expect, though, that your young dog will do it with any degree of regularity. He will nail the close lying ones, but not too many of them lie closely nowadays. Some men hold the belief that certain dogs have the power to hypnotize the birds and make them incapable of movement, but I am forced to differ with that opinion. My observation has been that such dogs beautifully nail those birds which gracefully submit, but that numerous other and more sophisticated ones get the heck out of there, but fast.

To handle birds properly your dog will need a lot of experience and probably a bit of help from you. You will learn to tell by his attitude whether or not a bird is lying close. If he stretches out until he looks to be not an inch less than ten feet in length, if every muscle is as tense as though it were carved from stone, and if his eyes protrude like doorknobs, you may reasonably suppose that the bird is not far ahead.

If, however, you notice a relaxing of tenseness, or an air of uncertainty in his pose, it is then your job to give him some assistance. If you can get to him without putting the bird up it is a pretty good bet that he hasn't located it yet. Take a few steps ahead of him to show him that the bird isn't there. Then go back and urge him on. You may have to move him by main strength, but once the spell is broken he will probably tear around as though he were suddenly demented. It is a two-to-one shot that he will probably put the bird up then, but it is a part of his education, and if he can't learn to locate them accurately he will never be much help to you.

Occasionally one finds a dog who is determined to get too close to his bird, creeping stealthily in until he has crossed the deadline, but your chance of owning one is very slight. Your job will be to get him to go in close enough, and it will be his job to learn to the exact inch where the deadline is drawn, and to not go a red hair farther unless the bird moves on. It is another part of his job to move ahead then, never crowding the bird but keeping in intimate touch with it by that miraculous thread of scent. That, my boy, is stanchness in the true sense of the word, and there will come a time when only that sort of bird work will satisfy you. I hope that you will own at least one dog who will meet those specifications.

I must call your attention, too, Jimmy, to the matter of sportsmanship. Being both young and human, your chief desire at first will be to kill grouse, and it will not matter particularly to you how you do it. You will want people to believe that you are a shade better than Annie Oakley when she was at her best, and you'll come home at night with two or three grouse slung from your belt rather than nesting inconspicuously in your game pocket. Burdened thus, with your gun under your arm and your dog at heel, you will swagger down the main drag in order that the gaping populace may get an eyefull of your own illustrious self. In order to do that you will need grouse, and so you'll gather them in from where they sit by the roadside or peer down at you from their fancied security on a gnarled old limb.

I hope you will not misunderstand me. There are men who love to still-hunt grouse on the ground. There are others whose chief delight is to go out with a barking spaniel and shoot birds the dog has treed. Either method is perfectly legitimate and fair, but you are planning to become a wing shot—a grouse hunting specialist. You will learn that there is no satisfaction comparable to that of cutting down a startled bird in the split second allotted to you before it gained protective cover, and you will learn that the bushwhacking of a sitting bird is going to leave you with an unpleasant memory and a wry taste in your mouth.

All game has certain definite rights. It has the right to perpetuate its species in order to assure a future supply. Game is a trust fund, Jimmy, held for the moment under our names, and we are entitled only to our small share of the interest. For that reason I hope that you will never clean up a cover so completely that there is insufficient breeding stock left. It takes a long, long time for grouse to come back.

Well, I guess that's about all I can tell you, Jimmy. You'll have to work most of it out for yourself, but you may have this consolation. You are going to have a lot of fun while you are doing it. There are other compensations, too. You will learn to love the crimson and gold of the autumn woods, and all the little feathered folk who pause in their fall migration to chirp a cheery hello to you as you pass. You will learn self reliance, and within you will be born the unshakable conviction that you are the equal of any king and the superior of no commoner. You will learn steadfastness of purpose and a gentleness that is in utter variance with the trade you ply. You will learn to make decisions and to stand or fall by them as a he-man should.

Jimmy, my boy, you are in for a happy, happy time. I envy you as I envy no one else in all the world.

CHAPTER 12

Gift Grouse

I disagree with the fellow who said "I am the master of my fate." Things happen. There was the time when Jim and I, during a fall of unprecedented low water, went, with our pockets bulging with No. 4's, up to Great Pond to hunt the sloughs and newly exposed weed beds for black ducks. We didn't find the ducks but we ran into the biggest concentration of jacksnipe that I have ever seen, or expect to see again. How we blasted our way up and down those boggy shores, spraying the whole landscape with shot several sizes too large, does not concern this story, for it is a yarn in itself, but it proves that, on that day at least, we were masters neither of our fate nor of the situation.

Then there was the time when Henry and I sat in a duck blind that fronted on an eelgrass bed which the ducks avoided on that day as if it were poison. We had huddled there for hours, discouraged and half frozen, when a squall of blizzard proportions whooped down upon us. With my hearing dulled by the howling gale, and my eyes closed by the assault of the stinging sleet, I was electrified by Henry's startled "Goddlemighty!" and looked out to see the whirling and empty void before us suddenly filled with clamoring Canada honkers.

There was another time when—but let's start at the beginning.

It was early October, and for a week Bill and I had been hunting woodcock. Not because we preferred it to grouse hunting, but because in our section of the country the first two weeks of open season seldom furnish good sport on the larger birds. The weather is usually far too warm for the more strenuous exercise that hunting them entails, while the birds, in the last stages of moulting, prefer to remain in the big swamps where hunting them is anything but a pleasure.

Because of these reasons we prefer to hunt the longbills for the first few weeks. Their haunts are restricted in area, and a hunter can look over a half dozen favored covers in a day and still be able to climb into the car when night comes. Then, too, the less wary birds furnish excellent practice for dogs made over anxious by ten months of inactivity, and steadies them for the more serious business of grouse hunting.

Thus it was that Bill and I made our way down the sloping hillside and into the alders which form the beginning of the Beecher cover. It is excellent woodcock country. The ground is soft and springy, and although it rarely exceeds a hundred yards in width it is nearly a mile long, encircling two sides of the small pond. Native birds breed there, and flighters often drop in during the fall migration, but there are no evergreens near it, or any heavy cover. Consequently one never finds grouse there— or no one ever did until the Memorable Day.

We had taken four woodcock that morning. Three from the Millbrook cover and one from an unnamed and inconsequential alder patch beside the road, and we needed four more to fill our limit. We had not hunted the Beecher cover as yet, but we were confident that we could collect the remainder of our quota there, for it was not unusual for the place to harbor at least a dozen birds.

"One of the things I particularly like about this cover," Bill said, as he dropped a shell containing three-fourths of an ounce of No. 9's into the breech of his 20 ga., closed the action and fed two more into the magazine, "is the fact that you always know what to expect. When you're all set for a woodcock and a pa'-tridge goes hellity-clatterin' out, it does something to your nerves that—Oh-oh! *Bud's* nailed one already."

I looked ahead through the leafy screen, and there, forty feet away and stretched out in a solid point, was his young black-and-white pointer. He was an independent youngster, paying no attention to what my setter was doing, and already convinced that he could find birds of his own and hold them without help from anybody. He had the fire and enthusiasm of youth, and the picture was heart warming.

"No other bird is quite so good as woodcock to work a young dog on," Bill said, as we went unguardedly in. "They lie so close that—"

WHIR-R-R-R! The air trembled as at least a half dozen ruffed grouse exploded like bursting shrapnel and went rocketing up through the pliant branches that swayed and tossed with the wind of their passing. They were gone instantly, while we stood spellbound, our guns clutched in rigid hands.

"Thunder and lightning!" Bill said at last. "An unbroken flock and we stood here like a couple of wooden Indians and let them get away."

"The nice thing about this cover," I began, "is the fact that—"

He grinned. "First time I ever saw a pa'tridge in the place, but we shouldn't have been caught asleep at the switch. Where do you suppose the doggone critters came from?"

"Probably a pair of old birds strayed in here this spring," I said. "If so, they did all right by themselves. A nice little flock of birds."

"Almost like one of those old time, honest-to-God bunches," he agreed. "Well, let's get after them."

The young pointer, as though the pervading odor of so many grouse was an anesthetic, still held statue-like, but Bill's chirrup broke the spell and he went around and around like a young cyclone. "Nothin' like pa'tridge scent to put pep into 'em," Bill said. "Where's *Bob?*"

"The last I saw of him he was working down toward the pond," I answered. "I'll look him up."

I found him frozen in a solid point in the last fringe of cover close by the shore of the pond. His plume-like tail was held high aloft, his eyes were bulging, his nostrils widely expanded as he inhaled the rich warm scent.

As I stepped in front of him a woodcock vaulted sharply upward as though propelled by a giant spring, but my shot charge caught it as it cleared the tops of the alders. A tiny puff of feathers floated from it as it collapsed and plummeted down.

Then a heart warming thing happened. After a dog of mine has gained plenty of experience I don't mind too much if he breaks shot to retrieve. If he is good he will not bump many sleepers on his way in. But I don't like to have a young dog do it, especially if the bird is only crippled. Too often he will get the idea that he can catch any of them if he only goes fast enough, and this young setter was just getting to the point where he was beginning to doubt the truth of that idea.

Therefore I was agreeably surprised to notice, even while I was marking down the spot where the bird had fallen, that the youngster was remaining steady of his own accord. Then it dawned on me that he was still pointing.

"Another one, eh?" I asked. "All right. I'll see what can be done about it." Tossing away the empty shell I slid another one in its place and went confidently in. Twenty feet—thirty feet—but no woodcock. The pup surely had a choke-bore nose, if he was still pointing. I turned to look back at him, and from directly over my head there came a tremendous clatter as a grouse left the top of an alder and zoomed away.

Had it chosen any other course it would have been safe, for the foliage would have effectually screened it, but it made the mistake of cutting out over the edge of the pond. Through the scattered fringe of brush I saw it for the necessary instant. It crumpled as I touched the trigger and struck the water with a mighty splash.

This was going to be interesting. I could make the youngster retrieve almost anything he could lift during yard training but, unlike most setters, he had a positive dislike for water. He had his share of brains, though, and proved it by going at once after the woodcock. My guess was that he had been pointing the woodcock when the grouse scaled down and alighted in the alder before him, and had continued pointing one bird by scent and the other by sight.

He dropped the woodcock in my hand and looked up at me as though to say, "Well, how about the other one? It's dollars to dog biscuit that you missed him."

"You'd lose your supper," I told him. "I killed him. But I'll take you on for as much as you want to bet that there's one bird you will not retrieve. He's out there in the pond."

I led him out to the shore and, holding him erect with one arm under his forelegs, pointed the bird out to him. He wet a forepaw gingerly and, holding it aloft, whined eagerly, then ran down the shore to gaze at the bird from another angle.

"Well, what are you going to do about it?" I asked him. "Leave him for turtle food? The wind is blowing him farther out each minute."

He seemed to realize this, for he came hurriedly back and waded out a few steps. He didn't like it and I could not blame him. In addition to being slightly moist the water had been chilled by the October nights until it was only slightly above freezing temperature. But whether it was cold or wet, the pup didn't like the idea of leaving the bird in it. He waded out another step or two, hesitated, then bunched his muscles and leaped far out. He shook his head when he came up, then raised it high as he searched for the bird. Locating it at last, he swam strongly out, seized it and bore it proudly back to me.

"Nice work," I said, as I stooped to pat him. He responded by drenching me thoroughly with a shower of spray as he shook himself, then laid the bird in my hand. He was not for sale but, just the same, his price went up another hundred dollars.

I stowed it away and was heading back into the cover when I

heard the report of Bill's gun, and almost instantly thereafter a
lone grouse planed down above the tops of the alders to my left,
tipped sharply upward to check its speed, then dropped into the
cover at a distance of not more than fifty yards.

The young setter saw it, too, and was off like a flash toward
the spot, while I picked my way more carefully along the boggy
shore. Parting the bushes a few moments later, I saw the dog,
not pointing stanchly, but creeping on cat-like feet slowly and
cautiously ahead. That black-and-white youngster was going to
make a grouse dog someday. In my book that careful, stiff legged
advance meant that the grouse, alarmed as it had good reason to
be, was stealing away before him, and that he was following its
every move by body scent alone.

If there had been a corner into which we could have driven
it, or even an opening which it must cross, the bird would have
paused when it reached the last bit of shelter, but here there was
nothing to check it. The situation called for only one course of
action, so holding the gun ready I hurried up to the dog, passed
him and went boldly and quickly in.

"Ah!" I caught a flash of brown as the bird left the ground,
but instead of coming up it zigzagged away as only a ruffed
grouse can do, low down among the criss-crossed trunks, dodging to right and left, yet making incredible speed through the
impossible tangle.

NO jacksnipe can perform such aerial gymnastics, and I never
blame myself when I miss that kind of shot. Perhaps it is well
that I don't, for I missed that one by a yard, and before I could
pull the trigger again the bird was gone from sight.

"Anyway, you did your part," I said to the dog. "And don't
look at me like that. I'm no Annie Oakley."

"Whoo-hoo!" That was Bill calling from the other side of the
run. "Whoo-hoo. Did you get that one?"

"No."

"So did I," he said. "There were four in that bunch. Three of them went ahead of me. Work over this way."

Sending *Bob* on, I worked toward the sound of Bill's voice. Presently the pup began to make game. Then still farther to the left I saw Bill's pointer angling toward him, walking stiff legged as he homed in on strong grouse scent. Somewhere between them the birds were lying. I swung sharply away in the first segment of a circle that would put the birds between Bill's gun and mine.

Looking back a half minute later I saw that the setter had stopped, while beyond him at a distance of not more than forty feet I could see the pointer's tail standing rigidly upright beyond a clump of fern.

"They're nailed," Bill said. "Watch out! I'll come in and put them up."

It was a perfect setup. With the dogs at two of its corners, and Bill and I at the others, we formed a perfect square, and somewhere within the magic area we enclosed at least one grouse lay. That is the part of the game that I like best. I love it in all its varied forms, but to outmaneuver a wary bird and get in a position where it cannot escape without giving me the opportunity for at least a chance shot is the acme of hunting pleasure. One can say to the bird then: "All right. Do your stuff, and if you are a better man than I am I'll cheerfully tip my hat to you."

There is something disconcerting about the unexpected rise of a ruffed grouse. The noise creates the impression of tremendous speed, and it has a tendency to hurry the swing of even the most experienced old timer, but when one stands with gun ready, waiting for a bird to rise, the illusion vanishes to a large extent. I proved it a moment later.

Bill, with gun ready, was making his way carefully along when all at once I saw the setter's head tip sharply upward and simultaneously two grouse thundered up through the leafy cover. Before it was ten feet off the ground I had my gun trained on the one nearest me, but I knew that Bill was almost directly in line, and so I waited for what seemed to be ages for the bird to move out of line.

Then I heard the crash of the twenty, followed by the sound of snapping branches as a stricken bird plunged through them. My bird had now gained enough altitude to make shooting at it safe, and I was just swinging on it when the thought occurred to me that there was a chance for Bill to make one of the doubles that happen all to seldom of late.

I was right. Still swinging on the bird, in the event that Bill missed, I saw feathers fly from it almost before I was aware that he had fired. "Nice shooting," I complimented him, as the dogs gathered the birds in. He grinned and then looked at me in sudden suspicion. "Why didn't you shoot?" he demanded. "That last bird must have broken right for you."

"No," I lied, for Bill doesn't like to have anything handed to him on a silver platter. "No. She was too low. I couldn't see her."

"All right," he said. "I believe you, only don't let it happen again."

When he had pocketed the pair we moved ahead again. *Bud*, the pointer, working altogether too fast to handle jittery grouse, bumped a single, but redeemed himself a minute or two later by nailing another one at the upper edge of the cover. Once more we divided our forces and approached its hiding place from two sides, but the bird was quick to spot the one weakness in our plan. It ran to the very edge of the cover, then took off across the open ground, so low down that we failed to get a glimpse of it.

We went on, and in a dense little thicket of alders and goldenrod and ironwood we flushed three woodcock simultaneously. We had forgotten that there were such things as woodcock, for we were inoculated with grouse fever, but somehow we each managed to grass a bird on the rise, and then ignominiously poured two futile shots at the third one as it fluttered sedately away. I made a remark relevant to the occasion but Bill seemed to mind the miss not at all.

"There's only one more woodcock due us anyway," he said, philosophically. "As far as I am concerned, it doesn't make any difference whether we get it or not. Let's go back and find the rest of those pa'tridge."

I do not know how a flock of grouse, suddenly scattered, can lose themselves so thoroughly in a cover where there are no large trees in which they can hide, but I know they can do it consistently. It was so in this case. Originally there must have been at least ten birds in the cover. From them we had taken only three, but an hour's combing of the area produced only two more. The first one slid cleanly away, but the other one, because *Bud* came crowding in too close to the steadily pointing *Bob,* elected to fly back directly over my head. I miss that kind of shot all too frequently, but luck was with me that time and I gathered it in.

"We'd better leave them," Bill suggested sometime later. "They're scattered all over Robin Hood's barn. Let's go and get our other woodcock. That'll balance our budget on them, and maybe we'll find a pa'tridge or two while we're doing it."

We went back through the run. A jacksnipe went "scaip-scaiping" away from a springhole, and from the rushes at the edge of the pond we heard the whistle and clatter of ducks taking wing, but we were half an hour in locating our woodcock. The dogs found it on the edge of the cover on firm, dry ground, and Bill smacked it down as it corkscrewed out across the open.

"That's that," he said, "and I haven't any fault to find with the day. We earned our woodcock, and the good Lord threw in four pa'tridge as a sort of bonus. Let's go home."

We worked back along the shore of the pond. A V-shaped ripple marked the course of a pickerel that was chasing a luckless minnow, while far down the pond an osprey wheeled and soared, then plummeted into the glassy water and sent the white spray flying. The hunters were certainly taking their toll from the lesser folk today.

We were halfway back through the cover when *Bud,* racing gloriously through the soft mud, slid to a stiff-legged stop, turned and crept a few steps toward the alder fringe and froze in a rigid point.

I wouldn't care to hunt birds without a dog. Of course I prefer a good one, but any dog who will occasionally give me a point like that will find a warm place in my heart. There was no guesswork about that point. He knew—and we knew—that he was locked up on a close lying bird. We went in carefully, with guns ready.

With a staccato thunder of wings a grouse hammered up through the hindering branches until there was naught behind it but the cobalt blue of the western sky. From the corner of my eye I saw Bill swinging on it. Good old Bill! Swinging fast and accurately as he had been doing for almost half a century. Watching closely, I saw the feathers ripple along the bird's back as the shot crashed home.

I thought, as I watched Bill stow the bird in his bulging game pocket that this had been a day to remember. The gods had arranged to have grouse where we least expected them. We had taken our toll from them but we had left as many more for seed. Perhaps next fall when we came back—

That's another nice thing about grouse hunting. There are so many places to which we are someday going back.

CHAPTER 13

Finders Losers

Anyone who has hunted grouse as long as I have usually has one spot that lives in his memory as being about the best place in which he ever set a dog down. Also he probably cherishes the thought that on some crisp October day in the not too distant future he will park his car near the spot and once more do business on the well remembered stand.

In wandering through northern New England I have found a number of covers that were outstanding. Three of them are superlative and I hunt them each fall. While they are not so good as they were when I first discovered them, hunting them has become a sort of ritual with me, for there is always the hope that someday I will once more find them full of birds.

The fourth cover is certainly equal to the others. In fact it may even excel them in all the things that go to make a grouse Utopia. Better than anything else I know, I would like to hunt it again, but it is doubtful if I ever will. The distance is not prohibitive. The road that leads to it is at least passable, and time is no problem. I would be waiting there at daylight the first morning of open season if it were not for one thing. I don't know where it is.

That, I realize, places me in the same category with the nitwit who buried the family jewels and then forgot where he planted them, yet each of us has an excuse. His would undoubtedly be that he was under a severe mental strain at the time. Mine is that I was scouting off-the-trail roads in New Hampshire—and a man can get as thoroughly lost on those roads as he can any place in the world.

154

It happened years ago when I was hunting with my old pal, Gene; God rest his soul. Yet I remember the details as vividly as though they happened only yesterday. It was a gray day in late October, one of those overcast days that constantly threaten a rain that never falls. I love such days. They are usually windless, and although the sun is hidden there is ample light even in thick covers. A cool dampness arises from the earth, and scenting conditions are usually ideal.

Gene and I were scouting new country. Grouse shooting was still good but the birds had passed the peak of their cycle and we did not dare the risk of taking too many from the covers we regularly hunted. So we spent a lot of time driving over half abandoned roads, turning at random and stopping to investigate every corner that had a birdy look. It paid dividends in two ways, for not only did we find fair shooting but we added several fine covers to our list.

Then came the great day. There was no hint of sunlight, not even a brightness in the clouds by which we might judge direction. As we were eating our noonday lunch Gene asked which direction I would take if we were starting home. I pointed back over my shoulder. He shook his head and said that, although I might reach it that way in time I would have to drive twenty-five thousand miles to do it. Home, he said, lay straight ahead.

It made no difference. Day was only half done. When darkness arrived we would simply drive straight ahead until we found a signboard which would indicate the way home.

After lunch we climbed a few more hills, turned a few more corners—and all at once we were there. We crossed a culvert through which trickled a tiny two-foot brook. On our left a sandy bank sloped sharply down to the dirt road. On the right the land dropped away to a shallow alder-grown run that looked as though it might shelter a woodcock or two. On both sides of the run there was a rim of white birches backed by a growth of thrifty young pines.

It was the alder run that caused me to stop the car; if it held a pair of woodcock I felt that it would be only right to drop in and say hello. I was sitting there, looking the situation over, when there came a sudden whir of wings, and a grouse got up from the crest of the sandy bank, flitted across in front of us, and went scaling off into the birches at our right.

"That bird is our meat," Gene said, as he opened the door and let the pointer out. He seemed to take the bird's scent from the air for he was after it in a flash. We pulled the guns from their cases and hurried after him, stuffing in shells as we ran.

Fifty yards in from the road we found the dog locked up tight. The bird, we judged, lay in a tangle of blackberry vines that was backed by the first clump of birches. There is no better setup in grouse hunting than that, if the bird gets up as it should, for the vines force it to come out almost vertically before it can level off.

It is a mistake, however, to take anything for granted when grouse hunting. Deciding that the bird lay in the blackberry tangle we were not prepared for any other possibility. The proper thing, of course, was for one of us to circle the birch clump where he would have a clear shot at any bird that broke through. We knew all that but we didn't do it. Instead we went in ahead of the dog, and at least four birds ran undetected through the vines and took off, close to earth, beyond the birches, while we stood there impotently, unable to catch so much as a wing flash at which to shoot.

Gene said, "If you are thinking of telling me what damn fools we were, don't do it. That's more than I'll take from any man."

The grouse, or so we judged from the sound, had gone down into the alder run, for we had not been entirely witless. We had known enough to head them off from their sure refuge in the pines.

Sending the pointer on, we worked down into the lowland. He immediately began making game and soon came to a solid point. Separating, we went in on either side of the dog, moving

quietly and trying at all times to have an opening before us
large enough in which to swing a gun barrel.

It proved to be a pair of grouse that the dog had nailed. They
lay directly between us and came out perfectly, a right and left
zooming up together and affording shots that a blind man could
have taken. We put them down almost before they had gained
the blue above the alder tops, but when Gene told the pointer
to retrieve them he hesitated, then swung around slightly and
pointed once more.

Again two birds got up, almost exactly as the first two had
done, and again we grassed them both with two shots. I have
had many experiences while hunting grouse, but that is the only
time we ever had four birds down at once. We gathered them in,
one by one, and by the time we had them stowed away the dog
was on point once more.

This time it was a lone bird, and single grouse often lie better
than where there are two or three; but the bombardment must
have shattered this one's morale for it got up well out of range
as we moved in for the kill.

Because five grouse in one small cover are more than one can
reasonably expect to find, we were unprepared for what followed. The swampy lowland looked unproductive, and the
pointer seemed to share our opinion, for he went back to the
birches and almost immediately pointed again. We hurried up
and, mindful of our previous mistake, circled him widely before
we closed in.

Again came the thunder of wings, and again several birds got
up together, flicking through the birch clumps and heading
down into the alders I took a snapshot at one elusive shadow and
missed, but Gene was in good form and he downed his bird. We
harvested it and took the route down to the alders once more.

Working cautiously, the dog soon located game, but in trying
to get around him I bumped a pair of birds. It was an excellent
chance for a double, but doubles on grouse have a way of being

the exception rather than the rule. Almost always something intervenes to rob one of the glory. In this instance it was a sprawling alder branch. I killed the first bird quickly, but when I swung on the other that diabolical branch grabbed the barrel with both hands and wrestled with it for a critical second. I shot, but I shot hurriedly, and the charge went where most hurried charges go. At the double report three more birds got up ahead of the dog—and Gene was not yet within range.

We regretted it but there was little about which we could rightfully complain. We had taken five grouse in little more than fifteen minutes. It began to look as though this was going to be an afternoon for the book. Grinning happily we went ahead.

There is a limit, of course, to the number of birds which may be found on one birch hillside, and it seemed that we had found it, for the dog worked out the remainder of the cover without once striking scent. When we came to the pine growth we stopped, for it seemed to be the end of the cover. Then through a little rift in the greenery we saw what appeared to be another open spot a hundred or more yards ahead. At once we started for it.

The young pines thinned and gave way to birches which rimmed another run. Had I not known exactly where we were I could have sworn that we were back in that part of the cover which we had just left. The same birch growth, the same blackberry vines, the same alder run. To add to the illusion, the dog pointed stanchly in another blackberry tangle.

Gene said, "Now wait a minute. Don't wake me up. I'm having the most beautiful dream you ever heard of. We're on some sort of merry-go-round. The dog points and we kill a whole mess of birds. Then round we go and it happens all over again."

"It is not going to happen the same way this time," I said. "Not if that point means anything. I'm going around to the other side of those birches." Making a fast detour, I gained a spot where I could cover the opening between the birches and the swamp. "Put them out," I said. "Put them out and see what happens."

He went in cautiously and a lone grouse hammered out through the tangled vines and rocketed up to the tops of the birches. Gene killed it just as I was swinging on it. "That's the one we drove out of the first swamp," he said, as he held her up for me to see. "I saw her head down this way."

We went on through the remainder of the birches but they yielded nothing. Again the pines closed in to the very edge of the lowland. We would have retraced our steps had it not been for the pointer, for as he finished a short cast through the pines he slid down to the edge of the swamp and came to an abrupt stop. We went in to him eagerly—and that wholly delightful cover yielded us another surprise.

The brook had deepened, affording better drainage, and the ground was firm and sweet under foot. It was woodcock country if I ever saw any, and my judgment was confirmed a moment later when we stepped up to the dog, for one of the russet fellows bounced on whistling wings to the tops of the alders. That was as far as he got, for Gene, a dedicated longbill hunter, cut him down with a fast, clean shot.

From the Connecticut Lakes to the seacoast there are many glorious woodcock covers in New Hampshire, but there are none of equal size which are better than that little corner proved to be. From rim to rim it might have covered three or four acres, but everywhere the ground was spotted with telltale, half-dollar-size white splashings, and pockmarked with the tiny holes the birds had made in drilling for food. It was a gold mine that no other prospector had found, and in taking our limit of eight birds we had no more than scratched the surface. Another limit, and more, had fluttered up into the pines to await the coming of twilight when they would return to their feast.

Events such as that linger in one's memory. All forms of hunting thrill me, and I have never spent an unhappy day in the woods, even when hard luck was riding on my shoulders and jiggling my elbow at every shot. But I still think of that afternoon as one of the pleasantest of my life. It is fine to hunt with a guide who can lead you to the hot corners and tell you just where to stand, but for me there is no joy quite like that of finding a new cover, hunting it, and winning or losing by my own best effort. I thrilled to the joy of it then, and thrilled even more at the thought of coming back again a few days later to mine a bit more of the little cover's hidden treasure.

Twilight was deepening in the valleys when we got back to the car. We packed the birds carefully in the game box, blanketed the pointer and started off in our search for a signboard that would point the way home.

We went back a few days later, but we couldn't find the place. Nor could we on the next try—or the next—or the next. Years have rolled past but my memory of the place is still vivid. I know now what makes old prospectors go back year after year in their fruitless quest for fabulous lost mines. The same thing urges me on. I'll find the place some day. I've got to, for thar's gold in them thar hills.

CHAPTER 14

Grouse Dogs

I wish I were twenty years old again and knew one-half of what I know now—or one-tenth of what I believed I knew then. If that happy transposition could be accomplished I would buy a bird dog—a grouse dog. I would buy her only after knowing that she was a genuine, sure-fire, honest-to-goodness pa'tridge dog. Price would be no object. If I knew one-tenth as much as I thought I knew when I was twenty, I would know how to get the money.

Then I would breed her to another good grouse dog and spend the remainder of my life in selective breeding of her progeny. I would have one objective and only one: namely, to produce that rarest of all commodities, a strain of dogs with in-born grouse sense.

If from that you infer that I believe real grouse dogs are al-most as scarce as the proverbial hen's teeth, you are correct in your supposition. My experiences have led me to believe that not more than one in twenty-five of the present-day crop would make the grade, even under the most favorable conditions. The majority of them would go part way, but the summit would still be uncrowded.

I love both pointers and setters, and I am human enough to overlook faults in mine which I would not condone in others. I would not give much for the man who would not stand up for his dog. Let me add that I would give considerably less for the one who forever and eternally sings his dog's praises. A very intimate friend of mine rebelled against that no later than last fall, and got scratched off the list of one hunter's desirable shooting companions by so doing.

My friend is a keen sportsman, an excellent grouse hunter and an exceptionally good man with bird dogs. He is sparing of his criticisms, but he is always fair and just, and his praise of a dog's work means much to men who know him. On the day of which I speak, he was hunting with a man to whom praise of his dog was as the odor of sweet incense. He called attention to the beauty of the first point—and of the second and third. Birds were plentiful and were lying well that day, and while the dog's work was acceptable it was never brilliant.

When, for about the tenth time, the owner grasped my friend by the arm and commanded him to gaze once again upon that stupendous miracle, it proved to be the last straw. He stopped short, planted his feet widely apart and looked the man squarely in the eye.

"Yes, I see it," he said. "It's a nice point but, ye gods, man, that is what he is supposed to do."

He was blunt—too blunt to retain friends, but he spoke a great truth. A grouse dog is supposed to point, but that is a relatively minor accomplishment. The pointing instinct has been bred into them for hundreds of years, and almost any tenth-rate dog will stand a bird under favorable circumstances. The artistry, the consummate skill which sets the top-notch dog apart from all the rest is evidenced by his ability to make the circumstances favorable.

It would be difficult to visualize a more thrilling picture than that of a stylish dog on a close point. The immobility, the tenseness, the age-old instinct to course the quarry held in check by the newer inheritance of standing game are heart thrilling things to watch. I love it, but better still I love to watch a bird-wise old dog handle a shy, running grouse.

Here is artistry raised to the nth degree. From the moment when he definitely winds the bird he is linked to it by that in-

visible thread of scent as certainly as any angler was ever connected with a fish by fifty feet of vibrating and quivering line.
His approach has brought him to the leeward side of the bird,
and there he remains as long as the wily old drummer stays on
the ground.

First bird of the season.

Through alders and iron-bushes, evergreens and more open
ground, up hill or down dale he follows, walking as stiffly as
though there were not a joint in his legs, pausing rigidly as the
bird rests, going on again with its first movement, following as
grimly, as surely and as relentlessly as fate.

He knows to a yard how close he may come and still not flush the bird. Sometimes when he has exceeded that limit by what he judges to be mere inches you may see him drawing back a trifle, so slowly that the motion is almost imperceptible, trying thereby to become invisible to the bird who may have spotted him momentarily, and which shows unmistakable evidence of being on the verge of departing the scene by a speedier and more tumultuous method of locomotion.

When the bird finally lies, usually at the edge of some opening which, because of its air-borne enemies it hesitates to cross, it is a soul-warming spectacle to see the old dog come to his ultimate point. His approach has been cautious but businesslike, for he is an artisan at his trade. Now there is a subtle change in his attitude. His point is full of an unquenchable fire: his body a thing of vibrant, pulsing life, his eyes rolling in search of you and beseeching you in an agony of appeal to hurry—and to make good.

In my opinion, a grouse dog, to be a real top-notcher, must be both fast and wide, but his nose should govern his speed, and his brain should control the width of his casts. The faster he goes until he strikes scent, the sooner he will find game, but it will bring few birds to the bag if the dog is two townships ahead of the gun when he comes to a point. If he cannot learn—and largely by his own volition—to hunt to the gun he is worse than useless.

I am also of the opinion that the inborn instinct for blind and unreasoning speed which so many of the present-day dogs with whom I have come in contact seem to possess, is a fault which may be controlled to a certain extent but can never be eradicated.

I have seen a dog win a championship in a New England classic, and later sell for a fancy price, after I had chased him for many a weary week and mile in the mistaken idea that some day I could get near enough to him to step on his check cord at the moment when a grouse flushed before him, but it was a feat which I never accomplished. When I at last pronounced him to be a hopeless case, the owner sold him to a professional trainer, and the next fall he won the highest honor in the event to which I previously referred.

The trainer assured me, with the solemnity of a supreme-court judge, that the dog was entirely cured of his tendency to bolt, but later in the following season I chanced to see him crossing a field which lay between two grouse covers. It was a wide field, but he went across it with the speed and careless abandon of a stray thunderbolt, and disappeared in the woods a quarter mile away. I waited a half hour for the owner to appear, for I was desirous of asking him some questions relative to his system of training, but I waited in vain. He was still searching for the dog two days later, in an area several miles removed from the place where I saw him. It is possible that such a fault may be cured, but my preference is for a dog in which it is at least dormant.

Quite frequently I have been guilty of making the statement that the brains of a good dog and an average master were approximately equal, but I occasionally find that I have been doing a gross injustice to the dog.

Last season a man came to me with the request that I lend him assistance in overcoming a fault which had developed in a dog with whom he had hunted for three seasons. The dog, he said, had previously been very stanch, but now he had acquired the disconcerting habit of breaking point, then working ahead and pointing again.

"Does he put the bird up?" I asked.

"Oh, no," he assured me. "No, he seldom puts a bird up, but he refuses to stay on point."

We went into the woods with him, and my suspicion was soon verified. The dog had grouse sense and he was in the process of developing it. He worked high headed and fast, yet he kept in touch with us and slowed abruptly at the first scent of game.

A half hour later, when I chanced to be out of sight of the owner and some fifty yards distant from him, the dog passed in front of me. His head was high in the air, his tail was like a ramrod, and he walked like a boy on stilts. In about three seconds I was behind him, and my gun was ready for instant action. I knew—and the dog knew—that somewhere a short distance ahead of that choke-bore nose, a grouse was stealing quietly away through the concealing underbrush.

We went ahead for perhaps fifty yards when all at once there came a shrill whistle from the owner. The dog stopped short, and all the tenseness went from his muscles. For the first time in years I broke my self-imposed rule to refrain from giving a command to another man's dog.

"Never mind him," I said softly. "It's the bird we're interested in. Go on."

I pushed him gently with my knee. He hesitated momentarily, his ears cocked as he listened for the distant whistle, and then he went ahead.

Twice in the next hundred yards that scene was repeated, but the owner was farther away now—and the grouse was nearer. The dog's posture became more tense. Twice he froze beautifully as the bird stopped for a moment. We were nearing the end of the drama. A little opening lay before us which the grouse, as closely pressed as it was, would not dare cross on the ground. Once more the dog froze into a thing of marble. I stepped up beside the dog, and the bird thundered up before me, exposed itself for one fleeting instant, and in that instant ceased to exist.

The sum of my knowledge is far from what it should be, but I know I did much for the dog that day. I would have bought him, but the price jumped beyond all reason after I had talked with his master for a few minutes. The length of my discourse was not curtailed for want of time, but rather because in a relatively few minutes I said all there was to be said.

A long time ago I was privileged to handle a son of *Prince Rodney's Count*. He came up from the southland where he had never once smelled grouse, but the first day we put him down in a fantail cover he handled birds as readily and precisely as though he had been doing it all his life. Although I did not own him he won a warm place in my heart, and left his indelible mark on many sons and daughters.

As a grouse dog he ranked with the few top-notchers of my acquaintance, but his inborn caution worked to his disadvantage in the abundance of rank scent in a woodcock cover. Singularly perhaps, I have never seen a real grouse dog who was equally good on woodcock. I have seen many dogs who seemed to handle them with equal skill, but they were not outstanding dogs. They had not reached, nor could they ever reach the pinnacle to which a few favored ones may climb.

The field trial dog has very nearly arrived at the point of perfection. Until some venturesome breeder introduces a smattering of whippet blood in the strain, I fail to see how their speed may be increased. Bird sense and stanchness are the rule rather than the exception, and if a man has the inclination and the price he can pick up fifty likely derby prospects in as many days.

If you are a grouse hunter, however, and have that much time to spare, just see how many of your favorite type of youngster you can find. Then, if you are fortunate enough to find a pair of opposite sex, breed them and start on the career I outlined in the first paragraph. There is plenty room at the top. There's money in it, too. Dogs of that type will sell. In fact, you may book my order now for a pair of them, if they meet the following specifications.

Breed: I hardly know. I love setters and adore pointers. I'll close my eyes and let you pick them.

Size: You are about to breed above-the-average dogs, but remember to keep them average size. Between forty and fifty pounds.

Endurance: Now you're talking. Lots of it—never forgetting that mine is not what it was twenty years ago.

Nose: Both barrels choke bored. Capable of winding a bird, by body scent and under favorable conditions, at a distance of a hundred yards. Pointing them in trees and across ten-acre lots is asking too much. Have seen it done, but it is not necessary.

Color: At least half white for easier identification. But I will not be too fussy. Am not buying them for ornaments alone.

Retrieving: The mere ability to pick up a dead bird—which I often have to find for him—is wholly inadequate. If necessary, he must be able to trail a wounded bird, and distinguish between that and a live one.

Stanchness: Gilbraltar, the Pyramids, Mount Everest. Give me something along these lines as long as he is getting warm body scent. After that, give me—please God—a grouse dog.

CHAPTER 15

Real Ones I've Missed

I am one of that school of feeble minded folks who spend a considerable portion of what otherwise might be valuable time in following a bird dog around. In addition, I have tossed and turned for interminable hours while I dreamed wide-awake dreams about them o'nights. Oddly, the dreams all have the same wistful quality about them, and they invariably fire me with new zeal to go out in the marts of trade and wrest from them enough folding money to take another whirl at what thirty-five years of dog buying has convinced me is the biggest lottery in the world.

Not always have I been so cynical. Born in an era when ruffed grouse were so plentiful that a box of shells was seldom enough to last the day out, one did not have to be too choosey in the matter of dogs. If an over-ambitious youngster, or a hard-headed old bulldozer bumped a bird, or a dozen of them, it made little difference. There were other dozens scratching among the beech leaves, or burrowing on the sun-flecked hillsides, and any dog that would stand game under favorable conditions would invariably get enough productive points to satisfy any man who was reasonably sane.

Then the grouse population began to decline, and as the decrease tilted the balance down on one side, so did my ambition to own a real dog rise on the other. Thus do circumstances alter our fixed convictions. What had once been an easily condoned fault now became an unpardonable offense. A grouse hammering up out of gunshot ahead of an incautious dog was a tragedy, while two or three sliding away under similar circumstances became a major catastrophe. Each passing day afield accentuated the need of finding a dog who could nail them all.

The better half insists that dog buying—or more specifically, my dog buying—is a disease. She is undoubtedly right, for rare indeed is the man who, having been inoculated with the virus, can long refrain from taking another whirl at the spinning wheel of chance.

Searching for a perfect dog is similar to hunting for a collar button in a bureau drawer. Nothing can convince one that the thing isn't there somewhere, and he will paw over each article again and again. He almost finds it several times, and that's where the difficulty lies, for it is this business of almost winning which raises Hades. Let a fellow pick an also ran for a few races, and he may become so disgusted that he will quit, but the fact that his choice loses by a mere nose in the last grueling dash down to the wire only serves to urge him on to wilder plunging.

I remember that I began moderately enough, with no premonition of the danger into which I was heading. I bought a grandson of a national champion who had won because of his uncanny ability to find coveys of quail. The grandson was a chip off the old block, and might have won for himself both fame and my undying devotion had it not been for the fact that there were no longer any coveys of grouse. They still continued to wander around singly and in pairs, but he was a covey dog and gave them no heed.

Like a well-oiled lightning bolt he went in search of those ghostly coveys; and if he failed to find them in one county he went to some of the neighboring ones and continued his quest. Given plenty of sea-room and a bit of bird sense he might have been worth half what I paid for him, but he was a dud so far as grouse were concerned, and we parted with no real regret.

I went off on a tangent then, playing other progeny of winners, and at last I hit the jackpot—almost. I bought a three-months-old setter pup of good blood lines. She was shipped to me in a berry basket and I had to shake the thing to find her. Even on the butcher's opulent scales she weighed a trifle less than seven pounds, and a man with average eyesight could easily read 14-point type through her translucent frame.

It was windy weather when she arrived, and for a few days I kept her in close confinement lest she vanish in a sudden gust. But one sunny afternoon when the wind had died I ballasted her with a full cargo of food, stuffed her into the game pocket of my hunting coat, and struck off for a neighboring run which contained a pair of grouse.

May I never forget the moment when I dug her out and set her down. She was a thousand miles from the southland that gave her birth, a homesick little waif who had never before smelled the acrid tang of our moldering Northern runs, but her feet had no sooner touched the earth than she was gone.

I suppose that by some lucky chance I had set her fairly upon the warm, fresh scent left by a cautiously departing grouse. An elixer of youth to even a crippled old graymuzzle, it still seems incredible that it could have exerted such an instantaneous effect upon one so little and so young. She went from my sight like a wind-blown leaf, heading due south, and it seemed highly probable that I would shortly be advised that she was safely back on the ancestral acres; but I did her an injustice. She was a bird dog, and there was a ruffed grouse somewhere in the alder run.

Heaven could offer her nothing else half so alluring, and it is my witness that she went to the bird as unerringly as a homing pigeon to his cote. When I found her she was peering, round-eyed, over one side of a rotted crisscross of fallen alders, and a grouse, with ruff extended and crest erect, was stealing away from the other.

When she was five months of age she was pointing as stanchly as any old veteran. The following year she would, of her own volition, hunt to gun in the thickets, and spread herself all over the landscape when the cover thinned out. She would handle a running bird as efficiently as though she had it on the end of a flyline, and would retrieve anything that she could carry from either land or water. She was the direct answer to my most fervent prayer, and a thousand dollars would not have taken her from me: but pneumonia did, and I was hopefully back in the market once more.

There followed several years of groping in the dark, but during that time an idea was taking shape in my mind. This thing of always drawing only average dogs could only be caused by something more than mere chance. Some sinister influence was behind it, and I began to believe I knew what it was. Common sense dictated that no breeder would sell his best prospects, but would reserve them until they had proved or disproved their worth. Obviously, in order to pick and choose, I would have to become a breeder. I wondered why I had been so dumb for so long a time.

So I bought a brood bitch, bred her and settled back to await results. They were not what might be accurately called sensational for she had only one pup. One is such an annoying number, for there is no chance for comparison or a weeding out of the undesirables. It was disillusioning, too, to learn that a brood bitch could be so inconsiderate. I had always supposed that they scattered their progeny around like a shotgun. Her second mating proved to be even less fruitful, and I realized with no little chagrin that it was possible for an unscrupulous dealer to not only cull his puppy crop but his breeding stock as well.

There was, however, a way around that difficulty, and although it was a lengthy detour I was young and could afford to wait. I picked up a pair of young females whose blood-lines were of the best, and once more settled optomistically back.

It was about this time that Del moved into our town to work in one of the local factories. I never did learn his real name, for it was unpronounceable, but "Del" was part of it and we called him that. In addition to his patronymic handicap he brought

with him as companions as heterogeneous a collection of play-
mates as were ever assembled outside a city zoo. Gophers and
white rats, a miscellaneous assortment of lizards and horned
toads, an allegedly tame skunk, two raccoons, a window-mop
dog of uncertain ancestry, and a gangling, long-legged setter pup.

I still believe that in another setting I would have looked twice
at the pup—and twice would have been enough. But his environ-
ment overshadowed him like a pall and blinded me to his obviously fine points. I was still conscious of him though, for all that
summer he paraded the streets of our town, disdaining the companionship of other dogs, and walking stiff-legged behind the
pigeons which angled warily away from his cautious approach.

That fall a friend picked him up for a mere song and developed him into the best grouse dog it has ever been my good fortune to see. Superlatives are commonplace in describing him, for
the grouse never lived who could fool him for a minute. As old
age began to catch up with him he lost some of his youthful fire
on points, yet one of my pictures of him, taken at that time and
published in *Field and Stream,* later had the distinction of being
selected by John Taintor Foote to illustrate in a *Saturday Evening Post* article his conception of what the perfect point should
look like.

Thus went another jackpot. At the time I did not realize the
enormity of the tragedy, for my young matrons were fulfilling
their destiny, and for a time they literally rained puppies. It
would be an easy matter to pick a winner or two from all that
number—or so I thought—which shows how exceedingly infini-
tesimal was my knowledge.

If a man has two prospects he may perhaps choose between
them, but it isn't so easy when there are a dozen or more. The
longer I looked at mine, the more confused I became. I was sure
of only one thing: there was one youngster who would never
make the grade. He kept strictly out of the rowdy brawls which
were endlessly developing in the yard, sitting owl-like on the

slant-roofed kennel, and staring solemnly down on the rioting mob beneath him.

He lacked spirit and dash and vim, which are absolutely necessary attributes in a bird dog, to my way of thinking: so I unloaded him on a down-easter who couldn't afford the price of one of the real ones.

You've guessed it, of course. He was not only one in a dozen, but he was also that one-in-a-thousand kind who go out and make local history. He was a bird dog, the only one in the lot, and I practically gave him away.

There may be worse vices than dog breeding, but I have never experimented with them. Moderate indulgence may not in itself be harmful, but sooner or later the time will come when moderation fails to provide a kick. One yearns for more dogs—and more and more and more, and unless he does something drastic about it his yearnings are going to be gratified. The ordinarily sane individual has no conception of the extent that dogs will multiply under favorable conditions, when nature is permitted to run its course. Rabbits are ultra-conservative by comparison.

Dogs filled the kennel yards, looking wistfully out through the zigzag meshes, while all the footloose and unattached dogs in our township came to stand outside and look even more wistfully in. It required no keen perception to visualize what the neighbors would eventually do, but by a fortuitous chance I was located within a stone's throw of a state line. Reason dictated that if I moved the outfit across it at once to one of the great open spaces, it would be better for the dogs, and infinitely better for me if I happened to be over there with them when the sheriff came to attach my property as security for the rapidly mounting feed bills.

Fortunately, too, my shooting buddy, Gene, lived over there among his several hundred acres, and such were my powers of persuasion that I induced him to take a look at the world through my rose-colored glasses. He did so, and at last it seemed that it would not be long before I realized my ambition: some-where among the hundreds of dogs we would raise, a real one would surely crop up. I cannot recall a time when life seemed more desirable.

As an addition to the nucleus of brood matrons which I already owned, we bought a young female in Alabama. She was sired by a field-trial winner and bench-champion, and she looked the part. She was a glistening, silvery white, and beautiful be-yond my fondest dreams. I felt an almost irresistible impulse to sit down and cry when we took her out for her first run. I had never seen a dog so beautiful and so gracefully light on her feet. She actually seemed to drift hither and yon like a bit of thistle-down.

I hope I may never forget the first time she pointed a grouse and, in the light of what happened afterward I know that I have not hoped in vain. We had been following her for several days, our guns ready and a wild light in our eyes, for we had sworn a solemn vow that we would annihilate the first grouse that lay for this million dollar's worth of silk and satin. Bird after bird had thundered away before her too bold approach, but at last it happened as we knew it must surely do.

No fairer setting could have been chosen, for we had come through a cover of birch and pine that drained into a shallow ravine. Along both rims a few sumacs and thorn-bushes grew, but the bottom was only thinly sprinkled with alders through which a tiny thread of brook ran. It was one of those magic spots where one instinctively knows he will find a grouse, and our pulses quickened as the glorious bitch suddenly slowed, then slid boldly into her first productive point.

It was worth traveling far to see. There, amid the soft browns of autumn, with the last rays of a setting sun slanting down to fleck her silver coat with splashes of gold, she stood, and all the fires of Vesuvius burned within her. I still will swear that it was the most beautiful picture on which I have ever looked, and it worked its magic upon us. Thrilled beyond all understanding by the glory of it, we stood there spellbound, our unwinking eyes staring widely down at her, our hands woodenly gripping our forgotten guns.

How long we stood thus I will never know, but suddenly the spell was broken as the grouse hammered wildly out and away from an alder clump only a few feet in front of the dog's nose. Ordinarily one of us would have either killed or missed the bird in the ensuing second, but so great was the enchantment that had been woven about us that we each did an unprecedented thing. For my part, I made no move to raise my gun, while Gene, set always on a hair-trigger, responded only by a convulsive closing of his hands and mouth. Trouble seldom occurs because of the latter action, but the first might well have been disastrous, for his finger was on the trigger, and the safety had been disengaged for instant action. When his grip tightened, the startled echoes crashed back and forth from the neighboring banks, while mud and water geysered up from a hat-size hole in the bank of the shallow brook, and then we slowly groped our way back to normalcy.

That is how beautiful she was. Although we both foolishly believed that we were going to coin a small mint of money from the sale of our dogs, it would have taken all that we dreamed of and a whole lot more to buy that one from us. She was the nucleus around which we were going to build a strain of super grouse dogs—but that, too, was only another roseate dream. Something happened to her nose shortly afterward, and never again did she point a bird. Bold and gamy as anybody's dog at first, her inability to locate her birds wore her down at last, and she went creeping about whenever she came upon game scent, distressingly aware of its nearness, but with no more knowledge than mine concerning where it was lying. I have had but few disappointments so bitter.

My name must top many a sucker list, for the trust I have

accorded my fellow man has always been simple and childlike. Otherwise I would not have fallen for the line of a Kansas breeder who had exactly what I was looking for in blood-lines, but at a price which still causes me to wince whenever I recall it. While I have no regard for the breeder's feelings, I nevertheless hesitate to discredit the name of a good dog, and therefore I will refrain from mentioning the name of the bitch's alleged sire. Suffice it to say that it was first in the WHO'S WHO of setterdom at the time, and that the queue of matrons who awaited his favor was longer than the maiden train which graced King Solomon's court. To add to the attractiveness of the proposition, this favorite daughter had been bred to another illustrious luminary in the galaxy of stars and was heavily in whelp. My check went out on the next mail.

If it had been daylight when she arrived, this story would have had a different ending, but she came on a night train, and the express office was dark and gloomy. Accepting delivery without question, I loaded the crate into the truck, and started buoyantly back to the kennels, where Gene awaited me with a lantern in one hand and a hammer in the other.

Holding the lantern aloft, he peered between the slats of the crate, said "Hmph!" witheringly, turned and went into the house. I have never seen another creature so strange as the one which the lantern light revealed. I like height in my dogs, but this one was taller than she was long, and her length was not inconsiderable. Her coat was a depressing, mildewed black, and she moved with a peculiar shuffling gait which I attributed to her delicate condition. All in all, she was the embodiment of as vivid a nightmare as could have been dreamed by Poe. Gene, who had come back to assure himself that he was really awake, shuddered visibly and retreated again to the house without utttering a single word.

Man may sometimes assist in putting the finishing touches on a grouse dog, but the once-in-a-lifetime specimen is born with

99 per cent of what it takes, and this mongrel bitch had it. She weaned her pups, then went out in the woods and, with no previous experience on grouse, made the best prospects in our kennels look like rank amateurs. Up-wind or down-wind, whether the birds ran or lay close, she nailed them with a precision which in another dog would have been heart-warming.

Despite her uncouth shape and ungainly manner of going, I almost fell in love with her, and wish now that I had done so, because love is blind. But it gave me a slight feeling of nausea to look at her, even when she was on point, and Gene was openly hostile. He argued that keeping such a specimen would cheapen the rest of the kennel, which was true enough, but I think he might have relented after a time had it not been for one of those unfortunate circumstances which have an uncanny way of popping up at the most inopportune moments.

We were hunting the bitch one day in an extensive cover where birds were scarce, and she was really getting out in her quest of game. Following at top speed behind her, we came all at once upon a slightly alcoholized but tremendously excited hunter who assured us as best he could, because of his palsied shaking, that he had come within a hair's breadth of being run down by a grizzly bear. Out of the tail of my eye I saw Gene wince as from a body blow, and I was just about to explain to the trembling inebriate the nature of the phenomenon he had witnessed, when the bitch swung back from a long cast and came once more into view.

Seeking to reassure the fellow, I called the dog in, but even then he was highly skeptical, and edged away toward a spruce whose branches were conveniently low. "Homeliest bear I ever shaw," he said and, so far as Gene was concerned, we had come to the point of no return.

"Either she goes, or they all go," he said, and that was that.

She was a real one in the making, but I sold her down the river. Now that a few years have fled, I am not sorry for my action, for I have come to the point where I demand at least an air of respectability in my dogs. It is worth a little extra to own one who is easy on the eyes; but to find all the virtues which are necessary to make a superlative grouse dog rolled up in one small satin hide is comparable only to trying to fill a royal flush on a three card draw. The thing is possible, though, and that's where the trouble lies. I'll take three.

CHAPTER 16

I'm Training a Grouse Dog

Until quite recently I have taken considerable pride in the thought that I was an average sort of person. My chassis is what is customarily designated as standard, and while mirrors often buckle and bend under the strain, I have yet to see one shatter because I looked into it.

I have two eyes, an equal number of ears and a fair proportion of my own teeth. My hair is still dark, and I have a lot of it, although it is not distributed as evenly as I would like, being prone to indulge in a mushroom-like growth on my chest and the back of my neck, but rather diffident about coming out into the open.

But in the matter of brains the machine somewhere slipped a cog. It rammed in too much wadding and not enough powder. I admit it with shame, but I have long since ceased trying to kid myself that I am mentally up to par, and if you think I am indulging in a bit of idle persiflage I can speedily prove that you are in error.

I'm training another grouse dog.

Yes, sir! After vowing that never again would I make that mistake, I have yielded to an unreasoning impulse and let myself take the rap for another two or three years.

Up until the present moment I have put in about nine hundred and sixty-six dollars' worth of time on a young pointer. For the past two months I have tramped some five-hundred miles through some of the finest grouse covers in New England. My feet are leaden, my legs feel heavy and lifeless, my throat is sore from issuing ten thousand unheeded commands, while my lips are pursed in a perpetual pucker which enables me to whistle without the loss of a split second. My eyes are strained and blood-shot from peering into the distance, while my ears have become as flexible as though hinged. I have learned to carry them cocked forward like those of an inquisitive jackass, in an effort to hear the distant sound of rising grouse.

Out of all the chaos and tumult, though, one thought comes to cheer me. Believe it or not, I can look any man in the eye and truthfully say: "Not once in the eleven months in which I have been fooling with this pup, have I lost my patience or raised my voice in anger."

The pup was six months old when I brought him home. While I was making up his bed beside the furnace I grew confidential.

"Young feller," I said, "This isn't much, but it is all yours. I'll try to make it a happy home for you. You'll learn to think of me as a companion and a pal, and not until you are too old to hunt will you realize that I have been anything else. You will thump your tail then, as you lie on your bed before the fire and listen to my footsteps, and say, 'Hah! The old man was boss all the time, and I never realized it until now.' "

That is the way I wish my dog to think of me: as a companion and pal, rather than as a terrible and uncertain-tempered god. When I whistle him in he must come promptly, not with his tail between his legs, and belly to earth, but joyously and eagerly, with his body doing an Oriental shimmy in sympathy with his vibrating tail.

It required three months of daily endeavor to accomplish this, for he was a shy pup, but I made it a rule to play with him every day, boisterous and breath-taking romps which lasted for a half hour or more. But invariably, before the completion of these periods, we paused for a few minutes of schooling: never any-thing drastic, but such simple things as holding a ball in his mouth, or any other thing which suggested itself at the moment. The idea was not to teach him an assortment of tricks, but rather to let him learn that good times and obedience went hand in hand.

I have fooled around a bit with professional trainers. Any one of them could have taught the pup in a few weeks what it took me months to accomplish, but I had something in addition which no professional trainer in all the wide world could give me. I had a dog whose eyes followed every move I made. I had one who would leave his plate of food untouched in order to be near me if I went into another room, and who whined broken-heartedly if I closed a door between us.

When he arrived at that stage his lessons lengthened a bit and became, almost imperceptibly, more businesslike. As he dropped some of his puppy ways and became more dignified, so also did his teachings approach that tone. Always, however, whenever he did anything well, we made a joyous occasion of it. We forgot dignity then and romped until the rooftrees rattled.

These were no amateur performances. We put on the gloves and went at it, hammer and tongs. It is true that this made him forget much of the lesson he had just learned, but it made him bold and fearless.

After six months of this the pup had learned a few things well. He would come in at my command, sliding to an abrupt stop when the sound of the whistle reached his ears, and returning on the jump. He knew the meaning of "whoa" and "go on," and I could direct him to some extent with a motion of my hand. He had not, as yet, smelled a game bird, but we had spent hours pursuing pigeons up and down the village streets.

On these occasions I walked by his side, moving ahead with him as the birds moved, pausing as they paused, and never once did we give up following the one we had singled out until it took wing. We made it a part of the game then to stand rigidly until the bird had disappeared in the distance, when we would congratulate each other on a job well done, and go in search of more pigeons.

When the first cool days came we began taking daily walks in the woods and neighboring fields. At first I used a check-cord on him. I know of no other method so efficacious in teaching a dog to quarter and to restrict his range, but if a would-be trainer ever needed tact and an inspired good judgment he needs it when he attaches a check-cord to a dog's collar.

I pause for a moment to recall my impressions of some of the dogs I have seen come from the hands of a few professional trainers. They have been taught to hunt close to gun in thick covers, and they will do so. They will turn at a spoken or whistled command, and never work beyond a certain range, but most of those I have seen will hunt with about three-fourths of their attention centered on their handler, and with the other fourth given to the all imporant task of finding birds. Too often to suit my rather exacting taste, they go about the latter task in an uncertain and furtive manner, the memory of a thousand jabs from a spike collar so firmly stamped on their brains that they cannot forget it for a moment.

There can be no question about their being under control or of their remaining that way, but they lack the boldness and self assurance that a good dog should have. It may be that I err in my conception of what constitutes a well-trained dog, but I know I can no longer find any pleasure in hunting with an over-trained one. Give me, if you please, one that is bold and self reliant—a dog who knows that he can find grouse, and who puts his heart and soul into the task. He will make mistakes, but it is as true of dogs as it is of humans that the one who makes none is the one who does nothing.

With these thoughts uppermost in my mind I snap the cord to his collar and we start out. If he gallops I check him firmly but never harshly. If for any reason he does not range out boldly I remove the cord at once, and do not use it again until he becomes eager and animated. I am striving for an effect, and I definitely know what I wish to accomplish. I am trying to teach him that the thing of utmost importance is for him to find game, but that it is my wish that he look for it within a reasonable distance of me.

By the time he has begun to get an inkling of my wishes it is October, and I proceed to give him an opportunity to fulfill his destiny. He has learned that the dropping of an empty pail, or a pounding of a board against the garage cannot hurt him, but he has not yet heard the report of a gun. I have a foolish idea that this fellow will never associate the sound with something which has bored him to distraction at a skeet club, but will think of it rather as something inevitably linked with the startled flight of a grouse or woodcock. Therefore I steadfastly refuse to shoot at the few birds he finds and flushes in his youthful enthusiasm, for he has not yet given me a productive point. He has blundered upon birds in his eagerness, and I am pleased to note that he stops instantly when they hammer up before him. That training on pigeons is helpful to him now.

Then, one day, as he precedes me up a run which I know contains a few woodcock, I see his head snap around as he snaps into an intense point. With gun ready I approach him quietly. His eyes protrude in startled wonder and his nostrils quiver. By this wordless sign I know he has a close lying bird nailed there before him.

For the last few yards I walk the check-cord, to stop him if he breaks, for this is to be a nerve-racking test for him. I stop as I reach his side and run a caressing hand along his back and find him steady as a rock. As I scan the ground before him I press him gently with my knee and feel him brace back against it. No need to worry about this fellow being stanch.

"Atta boy," I say. "Hold everything."

The woodcock squats in the birch leaves a mere six feet in front of his nose. So perfect is its protective coloration that I am a minute in locating it, until its beady eye betrays it and I am able to trace the outlines of its body. It sits there, with bill out-thrust, and regards me with apparent unconcern.

The dog trembles in his eagerness and I began to feel jumpy myself, for a hundred dollars would not tempt me to miss this shot, and I recall numerous occasions when the little russet fellow has laughed at me. Will he never move? I wave the gun barrel at him, and without a single preliminary movement he hurtles upward to the tops of the birches.

It is his last flight. A puff of feathers snaps from him and drifts away in the breeze as he drops earthward. I reach for the dog but he still stands statue-like, so engrossed by the soul-stirring episode that I doubt if he hardly heard the report which echoed above him. It has happened as I hoped it would. He has seen the bird start, and he has seen it stop in mid-air at the crash of the gun. When this has happened a score of times he will begin to understand that I am a contributing factor to the miracle.

We wait until he has relaxed a bit; then I order him on and walk beside him as we go in and look for the bird. He locates it immediately and again points stanchly. I stroke him and encourage him to remain rigid while I pick up the bird and let him smell it, and I shall follow this procedure for at least one more season. It is easier to teach retrieving than it is to hold him from breaking shot, which he will have a tendency to do if I let him go in after dead or crippled birds.

He has found and pointed a dozen woodcock before he locates his first grouse. A few have got up before us, well out of range, and he has had a slight brainstorm each time he came to the spot they had so recently deserted, but we have not yet found a close-lying bird. Then, as we swing out into a peninsula of birches which extends for some distance into an open field he makes a sudden and startled point.

In some mysterious way it differs from all the others he has made. They have been tense enough, but this one possesses some dynamic quality which they lacked. He holds his head a bit higher, his eyes protrude and roll wildly, while under his satin skin I can detect a tremor, as though ten thousand volts of electricity were circulating through his system.

There is no need to steady him with a command, for a team of horses could not move him now. I slide the gun from under my arm and move quietly toward him. His gaze seems to be centered on a thicker clump of birches a short distance ahead. I approach it cautiously, gun poised for instant action, but find no bird.

Stealing a glance over my shoulder, I can detect a difference in the dog's attitude. He is still stiff and immovable, but some of the fire has gone from his stance. I go quietly back and stand beside him as I have stood so many times before when we were trailing pigeons. "All right, boy," I say. "She's moving. Go on."

It requires all the will power he possesses to enable him to take a step ahead, but he accomplishes it and moves toward the birch clump with all the caution of a cat stalking a robin. There is one essential difference though. No sniffing the ground for foot-scent for this fellow. The young inebriate likes to take it in prodigious gulps directly from the bottle.

He is convinced that the bird must be crouching in that clump of birches. To convince him of his error I circle it, then push my way back through. He can hardly believe it, and comes up cautiously on rigid legs. Then he sniffs at a rotting stump, and his tail sets up a vibrating tremor.

I say, "Yes, she was there, but she has moved ahead," and watch him interestedly, for by his action now I shall know whether or not he has the makings of a grouse dog. He sniffs about for a moment in an effort to pick up the trail, and I feel a great sense of disappointment. Then he lifts his head, and his nostrils quest the air. Higher and higher he thrusts his nose, and all at once I am gay and light-hearted. "Atta boy," I say, happily. "That's the way to find them. Pigeons! Go on."

He works ahead carefully, and I walk by his side to make it as much like the game we have so often played as it is possible for it to be. Several times he grows cautious, and points as the scent reaches him strongly. On these occasions I get ready to shoot if the bird flushes, but I am inwardly praying that she will not do so. If he ever amounts to anything he must learn to do the job he is now attempting, and he must learn to do it with no help from me.

I am thankful that we have been given such a perfect setup for the first grouse he has pointed. If we handle her carefully it is more than likely that she will travel the entire length of the run. Then, when she has come to the last bit of cover, she may lie long enough to give us a solid point.

The shooting will be difficult, for it is a pretty good bet that she will take off across the field, flying not more than two feet above the frost-whitened grass, and the chances are two to one that the last fringe of bushes will screen her from my sight. Were it not for the fact that the dog needs this sort of experience I would not mind losing her. I sympathize with her, but I hope she will have one moment of bad luck.

We travel thus for a hundred yards, and come at last within gunshot of the birch run. For the last few steps the dog has been moving with extreme caution, and now he stops. He stands for a moment, then gingerly lifts one foot and slides it forward, and gradually brings his weight to bear upon it. He starts to repeat the movement, but pauses and stands there poised on three legs, while his nose reaches out and out until he seems to be twice his normal length. I bend over and run a steadying hand along his back and am thrilled by its rock-like hardness. This fellow is *stanch*. Then I straighten and take a forward step.

The bird could have won its way to safety if it had elected to cross the open field, but it chose instead to cut back along the fringe of trees. It tips upward as the shot strikes home, and seems to hang suspended there for a moment ere it plunges to earth.

We go over, and again I encourage him to point while I pick the bird up. I let him nose it then for a few moments before I stow it away in order to let him know that I am happy to share the honors with him. I pet him and tell him he has done a fine bit of work.

I pause then, for I know I am prejudiced in his favor. He has done nothing that any other good young dog could not do. Out of the dim, dead years I conjure up the pictures of two other dogs I have known: grouse dogs so far above the best of all the others that they seemed like creatures of another world, and hunting over them became a different and somehow glorified sport. Thinking of them, I look down at the eager youngster beside me.

"Son," I say, "when you have learned all I can teach you, you will have merely started to become a grouse dog. I'll help you all I can, but about 99 per cent of it will depend upon you alone. You either have the stuff in you or you don't. I'm hoping you have it, for much of my future happiness will depend upon the quality of your work. There will be some years when we can conscientiously take a fair number of birds, and there will be others when we must content ourselves with merely looking for them, and shooting with a camera instead of a gun.

"But, whatever the weapon, I can still have a mighty fine time if you will stick your nose in the air and go to them as a homing pigeon flies. You do that, son, and about five years from now you can walk the streets and be as snobbish as you like. The old gang on the corner will stand aside to let you pass. They will sniff at your trail after you have gone, and watch your retreating form with profound respect in their eyes. They will have reason to do so, for you will be a creature set apart from the common lot. You will be a *grouse dog*."

CHAPTER 17

White Lightning

Bill made a grab for the white pointer who, with the hair standing erect along his shoulders and neck, was halfway out the car window. *Lightning* is a big, slashing pointer, a bird dog to be proud of, but he is a fighting fool who goes around with a chip on his shoulder seeking things to annihilate. Bill caught him by a hind leg and managed to pry him back inside the car, still frothing at the mouth in his eagerness to do battle.

There was reason for his madness, for the apparition emerging from the open doorway of the sagging barn looked like nothing human. A Rip Van Winkle growth of red beard hid all his features except his bulbous nose and bright, deep-set eyes. His hair had known neither scissors or comb for months, while the overalls he wore hung about him in rags and tatters.

Bill clamped a hand over the pointer's jaws, thereby reducing the unearthly clamor to a muffled moaning. "Howdy," he hailed. "Any woodcock down in the valley?"

"Ayah," the apparition replied, coming over to lean an elbow on the open window. "Quite a bunch of 'em sometimes, I guess. Don't hunt 'em myself. I'm a hound-dog and rabbit man."

"Bill, you're strangling that dog," I interrupted, for his muted rumblings had taken on a new tone, a soft whimpering such as I had never before heard him utter.

Bill released his grip, whereupon the pointer sniffed ecstatically, wriggled across Bill's lap, his tail wagging joyously, and thrust his nose deep within the long red whiskers. Bill said he hoped to be relegated to the unquenchable conflagration if he had ever seen anything like that, and he was even more startled when

Van Winkle fondled the dog's ears, scratched behind them and recovered his hand intact.

"Nice lookin' dog," Van Winkle said. "Looks like he might be able to travel. A big, fast-goin' dog is what we need up here for rabbits. Snow gets so deep that a small dog would have to dig a tunnel. Got a Walker bitch out back that's goin' to make good. Likes foxes best, but I can break her of it. She's a picture. Want to see her?"

He was right about her being a picture, as I learned when we rounded the corner of the dilapitated barn and came to a well-constructed kennel enclosed by a six-foot wire fence. Although I am primarily a bird dog man, that Walker hound inside the enclosure fairly took my breath away, she was so beautiful. Bill's eyes, too, bugged when he saw her, but his interest was as nothing compared to that of the pointer. He is a big, tough character, but he fell for her at the first glance, and he fell hard. Miraculously he took on an airy grace and danced about on winged feet.

"I've been buildin' a crate for her," Van Winkle said. "Goin' to ship her up to Barre this afternoon. Feller up there's got a great rabbit dog. Figgered I'd raise a litter of pups from her."

Within the enclosure the bitch did a light-footed shuffle, then thrust her nose through the meshes of the fence in friendly greeting, and the pointer went into ecstasies of joy. Then he stepped back and cooly estimated the height of the restraining fence. Fences mean nothing in his life. He never bothers to hunt for a way through or around them, but merely bunches his muscles and zooms over the top.

"Bill!" I cautioned sharply. "Get a lead on that dog and let's get going."

Bill glanced around, then drew the leash from his pocket. "Looks like that might be a good idea."

We had spied this valley from afar while looking for woodcock, had found the rutted old road that led to it, and had bounced and jolted our way in until we had come to the end of the trail. It was the end of civilization, too, but the land sloped down into a wide valley that was woodcock country if I ever say any. We went eagerly forward, warmed by the thrill one always feels when going in to a new cover.

The alder runs were all they had looked to be from the distant ridge, but although we found numerous splashings they were weathered and dried. The always unpredictable woodcock had evidently left for a warmer clime. At the end of the run, though, where the first ridges rose to buttress the surrounding mountains, in a mecca of birches and wild apple trees, we found grouse. A lot of grouse.

Each ridge produced birds, and we might have had a field day with them, but the pointer was strangely inefficient. He bumped birds, and he passed within scant feet of others without detecting their presence. Never since his puppy days had he done such sloppy work. Then we lost him. There were hundreds of places where he might have remained concealed if he were locked up on a bird, but a half hour's search failed to locate him. Then Bill saw the light. "Oh, oh!" he said. "I know where the hellion is. Come on."

Bill was right in his surmise, as I learned when we got back to the kennel. The pointer was there, inside the fence, looking out at us with a sheepish grin, and the bitch was peering coyly over his shoulder. Bill pushed the gate open, dragged the pointer out and looked furtively about. "Let's get out of here, but fast," he said.

The next season we found both grouse and woodcock so plentiful that it was unnecessary to journey far afield, but I could not forget those half-explored covers, and twice, when we were within reasonable driving distance of them, I suggested that we go in and give them a working over, but Bill would not listen to it.

"No sir," he said. "The way I figger it, we were lucky to get

out of there without soakin' up a charge of bird-shot, and I'm
not goin' to tempt providence by goin' back."

"Nonsense," I argued. "Van Winkle can't blame us for it. It
was just an accident."

"Oh, yeah? Believe me, bud, it wasn't any accident. It was
planned and premeditated, and I ain't goin' back there, never."

Bill kept his vow for two long years, but last fall, after the
woodcock season had ended, he showed the first sign of relenting.
Grouse were still fairly plentiful, but the hunting pressure in the
better known covers had thinned their numbers, and once again
we were pushing out to some of the more remote places.

"You remember the dog cover?" Bill unexpectedly asked one
day.

I told him it would be a long long time before I forgot a single
detail of it.

"Remember up above the alder runs? Those birch ridges and
old apple orchards? I'll bet there's a raft of birds up there right
now."

I fed fuel to the tiny flame. "We left a lot of birds up there,"
I agreed. "I doubt if many hunters know about the place. We
could probably do business if we dared take a chance."

Bill thought it over for a half minute. "He'd likely be cuttin'
wood or somethin'. We might be able to slip in for a half day
without gettin' caught."

"When?" I asked. "Tomorrow?"

Bill thought that over, too. "What the heck!" he said finally.
"The old geezer couldn't do no more than shoot us. Or maybe he
figgered the guy up in Barre was careless. Looks like tomorrow
might be a good day."

Next morning we parked the car in a gravel pit a quarter
mile short of the house, loaded our pockets with shells, snapped
the leash on the pointer and struck off on a circular course which
brought us out to the alder runs and, eventually, to the birch
ridges and wild apple trees. Two years previously the latter had

been loaded with fruit, and grouse had apparently come for miles to feed upon their choicest delicacy, but now there was not so many as one lone windfall beneath the trees, and save for a stray or two we could find no birds.

Coming together at the crest of a ridge, we paused for a consultation. "Another beautiful dream shattered," I said. "Where do we go from here?"

Bill did not answer. His head was cocked in a listening attitude, and one hand was cocked behind his ear.

I heard it then, a frantic *yi-yi-yi* echoing back from the craggy hills and coming toward us at jet-plane speed. Then something small and brown and white flashed across the ridge beside us, towing, or so it seemed, a larger and whiter object from which came this wild and joyous yelping. They were gone from our sight in an instant, and only the sound remained, shrill and vibrant for a moment, then diminishing to a mere whisper in the distance.

Bill removed his hat, scratched his graying head, and grinned wryly. "I've bragged that my dog was rabbit proof," he said, "but I'll take it back. He—well I'll be teetotally damned! Look!"

I followed his glance, and there was the pointer within ten feet of us, his head cocked on one side, and an inquisitive ear raised as he listened to the eerie whisper which still came faintly back to us from somewhere down in the alder runs.

"Did I see that or dream it?" Bill asked, perplexedly. "I'd have sworn I saw *Lightnin'* hightailin' it after a jack. Listen!"

The faint murmur of the distant chase was taking on substance again, circling the lower edge of the ridge with incredible speed. Each strained yelp was clear and distinct, and as evenly spaced as the ticking of a watch.

"They'll cross here again," Bill said, and I could detect the rising excitement in his voice. "If it really is a rabbit, let's spread out and stop him." He slid the gun from under his arm and moved back along the ridge, while I went ahead and took a stand on a flat-topped rock.

We had wasted no time, but in those few brief moments the chase had drawn close. It swung along the base of the cliff above us, dropped momentarily into a hollow, then emerged and came straight toward us.

Like every other down-east shotgunner, I have hunted snow-shoe rabbits with hounds. I have hunted over slow dogs and I have hunted over others which were called fast, but I had never seen speed like this. The jack came into sight some fifty yards away, on a quartering course which would bring him along the ridge between Bill and me. His ears were laid straight back and he had his accelerator wide open. When an obstruction loomed in front of him he ceased running and became airborne, and in that method lay his only hope of survival, for close behind him, and emitting a strained yelp with each bound, came a white ghost dog that might have been a twin brother of Bill's *Lightning*.

Events crowded one another after that. Swinging as I would on a grouse going downwind, I cut loose and was conscious as I touched the trigger that I still had not taken enough lead. Immediately thereafter, Bill's gun boomed, its echoes mingling with those of mine as they bounced back from the cliff, but I knew that he, too, had missed, for the gay, mad music did not skip a single note.

"Listen to that hellion drive, will you?" Bill said, as he came over to where I was standing. "He's so fast that a telegram couldn't catch him."

He was indeed a hellion. His wild melody came strongly back for a moment as he zoomed down the ridge toward the flats, then lessened to a murmur which at last grew indistinct. Then, faint and far away, we heard the unmistakable sound of a shotgun blast.

"Somebody's out with him," Bill said. "Let's work down that

way and see if we can find out who he belongs to. He's my idea
of a rabbit dog. I'll buy him if the guy will set a half decent
price."

With the pointer at heel we swung down the slope, but before
we reached the place from which the shot had come we heard
the dog once more, far off to our right, and heading uphill
toward the cliff. We waited and listened to the chase flash along
above us, then turn and angle once more down into the lowland.
Again came the bellowing *"pow"* of a shotgun, and instantly the
dog's clamor ceased.

"He stopped that one," Bill said, ruefully. "He's a better man
than I am."

Again we moved down the slope, Bill leading the way, and I
following behind him. Presently we rounded a thicket of thorn-
bush, and Bill stopped abruptly, then backed up hastily. "Holy
cow!" he whispered. "It's him! Van Winkle! How are we goin'
to get out of this mess?"

"Not by running away again," I said, and to make sure he
didn't doublecross me I pushed him ahead and stepped out
beside him.

Van Winkle was there before us, dressing out a jack that had
made its last run. Slung to his belt in the rear was another one.
I called to him and he twisted his head around to stare at us,
then waved a bloody hand in greeting. "I like to draw 'em the
first thing," he explained, as he got to his feet and came toward
us. "You findin' any birds?"

We told him that we most emphatically were not finding any.

"Then why don't you hunt rabbits with me?" he suggested.
"Got a right good young dog around here some place. You'll
hear him open up in a minute or two. We could spread out and
get some good shootin'. That the same pointer you had when you
was up here before?"

Bill coughed, and emitted a strangled "Yes."

"Able-bodied dog," Van Winkle said. "Liked him the minute I set eyes on him. Got a lot of git-up-and-go to him."

Bill had been standing tense and ready to dodge a charge of birdshot, but now he relaxed a trifle. "He's a good dog," he admitted. "He likes to have his own way, but we get along all right together."

"A dog is no good unless he has a mind of his own," declared Van Winkle. "Now you take that dog of mine. He—Hark! There he goes on another one."

He was right, for once again that wild and primitive clamor burst out sharply from the ridge above us. "They allus swing past the ledges," Van Winkle informed us. "If we get up there and line up, one of us is sure to get a shot."

We hurried up the slope, but before we reached the barrier the chase had passed in front of us, circled to the lower level and was heading back once more.

"You git up there close to the ledges," Van Winkle instructed Bill, and I sensed that through their love for the same kind of dogs a mutual bond was drawing them together. "You'd better stay about where you are," he told me, "and I'll cut over that way a bit and try to head off anything that comes betwixt you."

The dog was still driving incredibly fast. Bill had no more than reached his stand when I heard the twin reports as he cut loose with both barrels, and then his exultant yell. "Stopped the son of a gun, by Judas."

His elation was premature though, for twenty minutes later he missed another one cleanly, although it failed to get past Van Winkle. Those ridges were alive with jacks, and in less than five minutes the dog had another one going. His scenting powers must have been excellent, but he had little occasion to use them after jumping his quarry, for with those steel springs he used for legs he could run any jack by sight in that open country.

I will always remember that afternoon. By taking what seemed to be a wholly unreasonable lead I managed to bowl over one of those hurtling satellites. Van Winkle, strategically placed, collected two that Bill missed, and then Bill made good on another one.

The sun was sliding down behind the hills when we decided to call it a day, and started down toward Van Winkle's shabby dwelling. Bill and the native walked side by side in their new companionship. The two dogs, as alike as two peas, followed each behind his master. I brought up the rear, a forgotten third party. Bill and Van Winkle were talking, and although their voices were low I caught a word now and then and knew they were discussing that once-in-a-million rabbit dog.

". . . . out of that Walker bitch," I heard Van Winkle say. "Only one she had, too. Just my luck. Could have made a barrel of money with a good litter."

"By the Barre dog?" Bill asked.

"No. Changed my mind and didn't ship her."

We had reached the house then, and paused for a moment before starting up the road toward the car. "You come up any time you can," Van Winkle said to Bill.

Bill said he'd sure like to try it again, but he didn't want to put anybody to any trouble.

"No trouble at all," Van Winkle assured him. "I like to go myself, and I'd like to have you with me. Besides, I figger that I owe you a little somethin'."

"You owe me somethin'?" Bill asked, incredulously. "What for?"

Van Winkle picked up a straw, stuck an end in his mouth and chewed reflectively. "Your *Lightnin'* dog got in with my Walker bitch."

Bill floundered around verbally, groping for words. "I—I— Dammit, I know she did. Should have told you, but—well—I figgered it was an accident—and—"

"It wan't no accident" Van Winkle said, just as Bill had said it two years before. He spat the straw out and grinned good-naturedly at Bill. "Liked the action of your pointer. A big, fast dog. Was kinda curious to see what would come of a matin' like that."

Bill looked at him. "You knew he'd come back, so you cleared out and left him to jump the fence?"

"Well, not exactly, Van Winkle said. "It's askin' quite a lot of a dog to jump a six-foot fence. Didn't know as he could make it: so I—well—I unlatched the gate."

CHAPTER 18

Woodcock Like It Wet

Did you ever have a stranger on a busy street corner hand you a century note as you hurried past? Did you ever have a pretty girl whom you had never before seen throw her arms around your neck and kiss you so fervently that your knees buckled? Well, neither have I. But I have seen something happen that rates with either of them for surprise and downright pleasure. Here in New Hampshire I have seen woodcock come back in old-time numbers.

There was a time when New England suffered normal weather —and I use the word *suffered* advisedly. Snow piled up to the eaves in winter and left every swamp a quagmire when it melted. June rains caused freshets which flooded the swamps anew. Rip-roaring electrical storms dumped their inch or more of rain each week, while the always dependable September line storm was good for an additional three or four inches. Farmers and rheumatic oldsters and asthmatic old maids cursed the weather with varying degrees of artistry, but the woodcock pirouetted in joyous thanks to their gods. Worms bred with a fecundity that was amazing and lived in the top inch of soil. The tiniest baby woodcock could gorge himself until he bulged like a pouter pigeon, while the parent birds could raise two and sometimes three broods in a single season. Native birds were everywhere, and when the fall migration occurred it was frequently possible to take the daily limit from any one of fifty neighboring covers.

Then, deciding it would not be outdone by the sunshine states, our eastern seaboard dried up. The Connecticut Valley in New Hampshire retained some moisture, and so did the Penobscot and Kennebec valleys in Maine, but in most of the coastal towns of the two states one could prowl the swampiest lowlands from July until November wearing his carpet slippers, and experience no inconvenience except a thick coating of dust. Woodcock, working like hardrock miners to drill through the sun-baked clay, became too worn out to care about such things as mating. They were committing racial suicide, but were so physically spent that they had little desire to improve the situation.

Year by year the situation became worse. Woodcock hunters became morose, blaming the bird scarcity on indiscriminate shooting in the Gulf States and Cuba, and considered writing their Congressmen about it. One Maine man became so distraught that he even threatened to vote the Democratic ticket in the next election.

Then someone knocked the bung out of the rain barrel. Before the ground thawed that spring, incessant rains flooded the lowlands and turned highways and byways into passable trout streams. Frogs and lizards and all manner of amphibious creatures migrated to high ground, and even took to trees to escape drowning. By the latter part of August the previous rainfall record had been broken, and then two baby hurricanes dumped an additional twelve inches upon the already soaking earth.

Gloomy prophets among the bird-shooting fraternity predicted—and rightly, too—that grouse shooting would become practically nonexistent. Unless they were equipped with plastic feathers, young birds could not survive those torrential downpours. The woodcock fanatics were almost equally pessimistic. Woodcock could stand a lot of wet weather, but unfortunately there was little breeding stock left. The woodcock, like the curlew and the upland plover, were on their way out. The only thing left, men said, was to hunt ducks—if the ducks hadn't all drowned.

Duck hunting is something I can always take a little more of, but I like to mix some grouse and woodcock shoooting with it,

and I do not like that early season warmth when all the black
spiders and birch lice in a cover let go all holds and drop down
my neck when I pass beneath them. Consequently it was mid-
October before I hunted up Bill to check the possibility of a shot
or two at something wearing feathers.

Bill said he had been out a few times, and the appearance of
his pointer confirmed the statement. His ribs were already showing beneath his satin hide, and his legs were red from briar
scratches. Bill said there were some grouse—not many, but some
—and he guessed the woodcock situation was all right. He had
hunted only three or four covers, but he hadn't had any difficulty in getting his limit—except the usual one of not hitting
what he shot at. Yes, he had left some birds in each cover. Na-
tives, he reckoned. When the flighters started coming he thought
we might get some pretty fair shooting.

Bill said he didn't know of any reason why we couldn't go tomorrow. It would rain, of course, but that wouldn't make any
difference unless it happened to be a regular cloudburst. His
sinuses were bothering him, he said, and breathing through his
mouth, the way he had to, he kinda got waterlogged after an
hour or two in a heavy rain. We would go in his car, he said. His
gear was all packed in it and it would be too much work to shift
it into mine. He showed the duffel to me. Raincoats and sou'-
westers and hip boots. Wet shirts and dry shirts and a multitude
of other garments. Enough to outfit an old-time Armenian pack-
peddler. The only things lacking were an aqua-lung and a pair
of frog feet.

True to form, it was raining furiously the next morning, but
by the time Bill arrived it had settled down to the light drizzle
we had learned to call a good day. Bill said that probably we
wouldn't have to go far. We'd hit the Jones pasture first. He had
left quite a lot of birds there.

We got into our diving suits, screwed on our helmets and
struck off through a still-unmowed field toward the pasture

which I knew of old; a gently sloping hundred acres of alder and
ironwood and birch, crisscrossed with myriad cowpaths trod
deeply into the blue-clay soil, and every one of them awash to
the gunwales. The pointer splashed ahead, dripping water from
every hair, and was on game before we had gone a hundred
yards. The bird, he indicated, was in an open bit of flatland so
flooded that only the tufts of bunch grass stood above the water.
It would not have surprised me to see a brace of mallards go
rocketing out.

"You take him," Bill said as we closed in, and I appreciated
his thoughtfulness in letting me start my season with an easy
open shot.

I shook the water from my glasses, shrugged my shoulders to
loosen the heavy raincoat, and stepped in. The woodcock came
out like a jacksnipe, not two feet above the ground, corkscrewed
around the one lone bush in time to avoid my first shot, then
whisked back behind it again as I snapped off a second. (There
should be a law against leaving a shotgun in its case all summer.
The thing loses all sense of direction, and has no more pointing
instinct than a St. Bernard pup.) I tossed the spent shells into
the lake, shoved two fresh ones into the breech and slammed it
shut. If the gun couldn't do it alone, I'd have to help it next
time.

The pointer splashed ahead for fifty yards, then went angling
eagerly off to the right through a maze of ferns and ironwood,
the soft tinkle of his bell coming clearly to us in the heavy air.
Then the tinkle ceased. Slipping and sliding through the mirey
clay, we crashed over to the dog. That is one of the things I like
about woodcock shooting. Unless the bird had been recently
flushed you could go in to a point accompanied by the United
States Marine Band in full blast, and it would pay no more attention to the noise than it would to the wind soughing in the
treetops.

The woodcock was lying in a thicket of iron bushes some

thirty feet in diameter, which I circled to drive the bird to Bill. It came up above the tangle as it was supposed to do before it levelled off. Dry shooting, I killed it twice before Bill mowed it down. There was nothing difficult about woodcock shooting. Nothing at all. Why, a blind man could—

Another bird came up exactly as the first had done, towering aloft on whistling wings. I fumbled the safety, found it again with groping thumb, swung hastily and punched two ragged holes through the enveloping mist, after which Bill methodically added the bird to his collection.

"You should credit me with an assist on that play," I said, while we were waiting for the pointer to retrieve. "I kept her headed your way."

Bill grinned and said there was a bunch of small pines over that way that it might pay us to look into. He'd flushed four or five grouse from it the last time he was here. He thought they were using the place as a shelter from the rain. They might be there now.

They were there, all right, but not for long. The dog had just begun questing the air when I heard the first whirr of wings, followed by several more in quick succession. These grouse, bred and raised in the outskirts of a busy little city knew what the rasp of a raincoat on wet bushes meant. They got out of there pronto at a good fifty yard range. Three had broken to the left on a course which would carry them deep in the cover, but the fourth had elected to fly toward the field we had crossed on our way in. It seemed unlikely that he would cross it. He would choose rather to pitch down in the thickets which crowded close up to the stonewall boundary. We went after him.

A hundred yards ahead, the dog picked up scent and began walking on eggs. "Get out in the field," Bill whispered, and I circled wide to do it, although I was at a loss to know what good I could do the cause after I got there. I might, I thought bitterly, throw the gun away and arm myself with stones from the top of the wall. Certainly I couldn't shoot in the general direction of Bill and the dog.

The pointer was frozen solidly now, in plain sight and within thirty feet of the wall. He was headed straight toward me, and I knew that the bird must surely lie between us. I pushed the gun ahead and stepped up on the wall, and as I did so the grouse came out from almost' beneath my feet and leveled off in a straight line. A beautiful, beautiful opportunity except for the fact that it was flying directly toward Bill's head. Standing there, I saw the Old Master deliberately turn his back to me and fold the grouse cleanly as it hurtled past him for an easy straight-away shot. Bill, I thought sourly, was certainly being frugal with his ammunition this morning.

We slogged back through the quagmire to woodcock country again, slipping and sliding at every little hillock and hollow, and balancing ourselves like tightrope walkers. Here some pasture pines, too gnarled and knotty for cutting, had been uprooted by the embryo hurricanes, and close to the impenetrable tangle of their interwoven branches the pointer once more came to a stand. We skirted the blowdown, looking for a way in and finding none. Then, while Bill stood guard, I hurled splinters from the wreckage toward strategic spots among the barrier. At last I got results, and the russet fellow came boiling up through the tangle like an angry hornet from its nest, safely out of Bill's sight, but showing me an occasional flash of brown above the branches.

I was unprepared and off balance, but somehow I managed to squeeze off a shot in what I thought was the general direction of the bird, then cursed myself for my folly. Any man who accepted chances like that was a tripleplated fool. It did nothing to improve his shooting, and there was always the chance that a stray shot would wound the bird and it would get away to die a lingering death. One should school himself to— Well! by golly— There was the pointer, coming in with the bird. Show me the young squirt who could make a shot like that. The old man was the same hot stuff he used to be. Just a few rusty hinges that needed limbering up. Bring on your woodcock.

Ten minutes later the pointer bumped a bird while we were still out of gunshot. We watched it far into the distance before it banked sharply and fluttered down. "Right where we were goin'," Bill said. "A hot corner over there. I don't know why. It's just like all the rest of the cover so far as I can tell, but the birds know the difference."

I knew that he was right, for I remembered one cover which I used to hunt. It was so big that it required nearly a half day to cover it all and, so far as I was able to determine, each part of it was like all the rest. But day after day, and season after season, the woodcock would invariably be found in certain small areas of their choice and, unless I had driven a bird there, I could never find one anywhere else.

The pointer knew where we were going and he struck off at a pace which brought a sharp reprimand from Bill. A good dog, that pointer, with five busy seasons behind him, which is the way good ones are made. He slowed his gait to ours, covering the ground on each side, until we had travelled a hundred or more yards.

"That bird ought to be right here somewhere," Bill said and, as though to prove his master couldn't be wrong, the pointer whipped around and stretched out gloriously. Again it was open country, with only a young swamp maple here and there for a hazard. We separated and went in. Three woodcock got up simultaneously, one swinging to the left for Bill, another one going straight away from me, and the third one, gaining altitude with every wingbeat, coming directly back overhead.

From somewhere back in the glorious days when we hunted grouse for sport, and woodcock principally for target practice, memory surged. This was one that we had figured out long ago. I swung on the first one who was going straightway, saw feathers fly, then turned and bounced the overhead bird a foot higher before it plummeted down.

Bill came back grinning, holding his bird in his hand. "Kinda made connections all around that time," he said. "Same three that was here the other day, probably. At any rate, I missed three here."

That is one of the many reasons why I like Bill. He plays his part down rather than up, and the shots that he tells you about in detail are usually the ones he missed. "There he was," he will say, "goin' through a place as clear as a cement road, and danged if I didn't miss him twice. Guess it's about time for me to hang the old gun over the fireplace and call it a day."

We went on again, the dog reaching out in his casts, but no farther than we could hear the tinkling bell. Five minutes later it stopped, chimed lightly once or twice and then was silent again. No matter how many times that happens, the sudden muting of the silvery murmur never loses its thrill. Muscles flex involuntarily and the heart steps up the tempo of its beat.

It was a lone bird and I missed it ingloriously, but it made only a short flight and Bill gathered it in a few minutes later. "I've filled," he said, "and you've got one to go. We ought to pick that one up on the way out. It's most noon, and I figgered on eatin' a hot dinner today."

For a time I thought we might not find that last one so easily, but the pointer located it when we were almost out of the woods. Miraculously, I killed it. Here were the old days back again. Two limits in less than three hours. With nature cooperating a bit, the longbill could more than hold its own.

"They're queer critters," Bill said, as we climbed the wall. "Always find 'em on high ground in a dry year, but when everything is flooded in the swamps you'll find 'em paddlin' around in it." Again he was right. I recalled that in those Sahara years just past, the only woodcock we found were up on the ridges among the popples and birches.

"I sorta hoped we wouldn't do quite so well," Bill said, as we walked out to the car. "I wanted to get down to the flats this afternoon. I left a passel of birds down there. And the river cover is alive with 'em too. Well, I'll set around the stove this afternoon and dry out a bit."

The noon whistles were blowing as we shed our raincoats outside the car. Bill climbed in and switched the radio on.

"Thought I'd get the weather report," he said, "although I know what it'll be. They've cut a record and play it every day. Saves the announcer's voice that way."

He could have been right, for the metallic voice droned out the same doleful dirge. "Heavy rains tonight over much of northern New England, clearing tomorrow morning in the interior but with intermittent showers along the coast.

"Intermittent showers," Bill said. "Looks like tomorrow might be a danged good day to go woodcock huntin'. What say we try it?"

I said—but why should I elaborate. I'm sane, or at least as sane as most woodcock hunters. You know what my answer was.

CHAPTER 19

Secrets of a Grouse Hunter

"You want No. 8 shot?" the storekeeper said incredulously. "Who ever heard of using 8's for grouse? Nobody shoots anything smaller than 6's."

"Well, I do," I said. "I packed a box of 6's by mistake this morning and they're too large, at least in a cylinder bore. There are too many holes in the pattern."

The storekeeper looked at me pityingly over his glasses. "There ain't nobody knows nothin' about pa'tridge huntin' any more," he grumbled. "Not since Sam Smithers quit. There was a bird hunter for ya. Had a little camp up there in the hills and he moved right in with the pa'tridge each fall. Kept track of 'em so close that he knew right where they were every minute of the time. When the season opened he just went right out and collected 'em. Didn't even use a dog."

"How did he find the cripples?" I asked.

"He didn't have no cripples," the storekeeper said. "He used No. 6 shot and he killed 'em dead."

"Do you mean that he killed them all?"

"That's what I'm tellin' ya," he said. "If you know where they are, you know where they're goin' to git up. So you use 6's and point the gun right at 'em. There ain't nothin' to it."

"Where does this phenomenon live?" I inquired. "There's a man I've got to meet."

"Can't be done," the storekeeper said. "Sam's gone to glory. Died a couple of years back."

I knew better. Sam Smithers is not dead. He pops up regularly in almost every county of every state north of the Mason-

Dixon line. And among grouse hunters his prowess always grows with the telling. He never uses a dog, frequently shoots nonchalantly from the hip, makes triples and doubles consistently, and never—repeat, never—misses a bird. But nobody ever gets to see him do these things.

Reputations like that are easy to win—or lose. I know, for I was a Sam Smithers for one afternoon. A dog-trainer friend swore until his death that I was the best wing shot in seventeen counties.

He had put the finishing touches on a promising young pointer and invited me to watch her do her stuff. It was blowing a gale when we started out, and though we knew that conditions were impossible for the dog we went on. The birds were jittery in the mighty wind, watching alertly from high places and taking off at their first glimpse of the dog. Although she did not make a productive point, I got possible chances at five birds, at that time the limit. I threw one hurried snapshot at each—and killed all five with a run of luck that still astounds me.

Despite my modest disavowals, the trainer was convinced that I always shot that way, and spread the news over half of New Hampshire. He couldn't have been more wrong. If I could end a season with an average of one bird for every three shots, I'd be a proud man. There's a special niche waiting in the Hall of Fame for the grouse hunter who can average one in two.

No one need feel ashamed at missing even an unobstructed and straightaway shot. A ruffed grouse is fast. His getaway through a tangle of hindering trees cannot be excelled by any native game bird. Besides, the disconcerting thunder of his wings makes paralytics of all but the seasoned wing shot, and affects even him more often than he cares to admit.

He knows that he should swing toward the sound at the first whir of wings, mounting his gun as he turns. You can bet, though, that on those days when the birds are getting the jump on him it is because of the common error of trying to find his

target before he goes into action. Sure, he loses only a split
second—but split seconds are vital when Old Ruff decides that
'most any place is better than here.

When a grouse gets up at close range and flies in the open he
is not a difficult target. He is relatively large as game birds go,
and compact, with none of the deceptive length of the pheasant.
And when caught in the open he flies a practically straight
course. Trouble is, he seldom presents an open shot if there is a
friendly bush or tree to protect his getaway.

That raises the question: does a grouse deliberately try to put
an obstruction between himself and a hunter? Some say he does
not, arguing that the tree or bush is in his way and he flies
around it. I believe otherwise. The greatest enemies of grouse
are the accipiter hawks. From early spring until late fall they
prey upon him, and are the chief reason why he never ventures
into open fields. All accipiters can outfly him, and his only
chance to escape is to put every possible obstruction between
himself and his pursuer. In time he learns that man is also his
enemy, and he instinctively uses the tree-dodging method to
elude him.

The grouse nesting period lasts for two or three months. The
nests are always located on land high enough to escape spring
floods, and usually in fairly open growths. The young birds,
numbering from eight to twelve, are voracious feeders, consum-
ing both insects and greenery.

When hot weather comes the flocks move into neighboring
swamps and shallow runs, where they stay during the summer
months. But by hunting season most birds have left the deep
swamps. Many stay along the edges, but the grouse's tendency is
to seek higher ground and its ample food. Blackberries, rasp-
berries, blueberries and grapes are staples; so are wintergreen
berries and leaves, thorn apples and barberries. Mushrooms help
fill in, and apples—particularly sweet apples—have an irresistible appeal. Many a smart old dog comes to a point whenever he

A stonewall, an apple tree and his royal highness.

nears an apple tree in grouse cover. He knows there will be a bird near it.

But no matter how right a cover looks, you can be sure it will not be productive if there isn't a solid background of evergreens somewhere nearby. Stands of spruce, pine or hemlock are the grouse's safe retreat when danger threatens. With his protective coloration he can instantly become a weathered and elongated stub on a sturdy limb or an inconspicuous protuberance close against the trunk. Many an owl or red-eyed hawk has spent interminable hours waiting for him to make a betraying move as small as the winking of an eye, and have waited in vain. Unless his body is outlined against the sky, Old Ruff is hard to find.

For a few weeks when the first hint of frost is in the air the young birds are afflicted with a wanderlust that may stem from a prehistoric migration pattern. Whatever the reason—or lack of it—the grouse make weird cross-country flights, crossing big open fields, even crashing through windows or against houses.

Trying to find new covers by marking down a bird's flight during this so-called crazy season is as profitless as chasing rainbows. But later in the year it is good policy to follow any bird you see flying—even walking—for no apparent reason. He may lead you to a nice little jackpot. I know of no signal that grouse have for calling the clan together, but I'm convinced there is one.

Only a signal of some sort could explain an experience I had a few years ago. We had combed a particularly good cover without finding even one of the dozen or more birds it usually held. Baffled, we got into the car and started for another cover. We had gone perhaps three hundred yards when I saw a lone bird fly across the road some distance ahead.

On a hunch we went after her. It was swampy land, the most unlikely cover for midseason, but in a short time we came to a tangle of high-bush blueberries on which some late ripening fruit still hung.

Almost at once the dog was on point, and the next hour was as interesting as I have ever spent. Apparently every bird in the neighborhood had been summoned to the feast, and they lay like woodcock before the dog. It was one of the few times we each bagged our limit in one cover, leaving plenty more for seed. Perhaps the concentration was mere happenstance, but I believe that the lone bird I saw received some signal from the flock.

Similarly, birds that wander across the road in front of a car are on their way to someplace and it is often more profitable to follow them than to shoot them. I have found dozens of hot corners by trailing such birds, and it is the small corners that usually produce the most grouse.

Ruffed grouse are not exceptionally early risers, and the supercharged fellow who insists on getting into the woods in the half-light of early morning will accumulate little more than a thorough drenching for his labor. He may occasionally find a lone bird that is only half awake, but the great majority of them are still hugging their roosts and awaiting the full light that would reveal their enemies.

Even when food is abundant, all grouse wander over their chosen range, which seldom exceeds a quarter mile. In the morning they begin feeding lightly near the conifers where they have spent the night. If the day is fair, they wander to a sunny sidehill and loll in a dust bath for an hour or two. Then, as the sun begins to lower, they start the serious business of stoking their boilers against the long hours of darkness. In all the years I have hunted grouse I have never taken one with a full crop before the late hours of the afternoon.

So hunt the edges of a stand of conifers in the morning, work out into the more open runs and alders in the afternoon, and comb the highlands again as the day draws to a close. Many a man who hunts a cover late in the day is at a loss to know why it contains no birds, when he found a nice flock there a few mornings before. It's just that the morning cover was one the birds passed through on their way to a preferred spot. Ruff's wanderings may seem purposeless, but he knows definitely where he is going, and the better the hunter understands the birds habits, the greater are his chances for success.

One learns after a time to identify good cover wherever he sees it. Take an oldtimer with you in your car and drive through a country new to you, and the old master can tell pretty accurately whether or not you will find birds in any cover you choose to hunt. He probably does not know why he knows, but some acquired sixth sense tells him the answer, and he will be right a surprising number of times.

What should an ideal cover be like? First, there should be a big stand of conifers, broken by a few clearings and backed by an extensive area of lowlands and hardwood growth. Look for a brook trickling down through the lowland to open country. Here soil erosion has formed a wide but shallow gully or ravine. Alders grow alongside the brook in the bottom, but the sloping sides are lined with birches, a few scattered apple trees and enough juniper and blackberry vines to afford ample ground cover. The conifers and the swamp form a huge reservoir from which the grouse trickle down to replace those who guessed wrong a few days earlier.

There are those who prefer to hunt grouse without a dog. That's their privilege. My bet is that they hunt in the north woods, where the birds are uneducated, or have never hunted over a good dog. I'll venture to say that in a season of hunting a dog of even average ability will double one's chances. If the dog retrieves—and all dogs can be taught to do so—he will bring in birds that the hunter thought were clean misses, and find the broken winged birds that might otherwise be lost.

I hunt with a pointing dog, but I have no preference in breeds. Of the two top dogs I ever shot over, one was a pointer, the other a setter. If I could not have a pointing dog, I'd settle for a spaniel and keep him at heel until a job of retrieving was called for. He would help me bring home more birds and to a large extent spare me the remorse that a sportsman feels when he must leave wounded game to die a lingering death.

Because Ruff is fast on the getaway, a hunter is best equipped with a light gun. Of course lightness is relative. A brawny young giant might effectively use a gun that a smaller man could hardly bring to his shoulder, but even the big man could use a lighter weapon more effectively. The middleaged man who shoots the 12-bore that he used in his twenties is usually over-gunned. He may be the same old Deadeye Dick when he kicks one out from in front of the dog, but when the target is a brown bullet hurtling through a ten-foot opening he just can't get there in time to do business.

A shorter barrel speeds up the swing, but a gun that is a pound or two lighter can make all the difference in the world. Naturally a reduction in weight sharpens recoil and calls for a lighter load, but the difference in shot count is compensated for by the added speed in getting into action. The fast handling gun also lets the hunter take a second, make-sure look at those all-too-infrequent good chances so easily missed.

My present grouse exterminator is a side-by-side 20-gauge. It is a good gun and it has killed a lot of birds for me. I like it. I have another and—I hope—final gun on the drafting board. It will be a 12-gauge side-by-side with 26-inch barrels bored cylinder and full. Two triggers, of course. A straight grip stock with $2\frac{1}{2}$-inch drop at heel and $1\frac{1}{2}$ on a well rounded comb. Weight not an ounce over $6\frac{1}{2}$ pounds.

Why 12-gauge? Well, grain for grain of powder, the recoil seems to be less in a 12 than in a 20. I can take all that any gun can hand me, but I don't like it, and when one is conscious of an unpleasant recoil he is not in a frame of mind for good shooting. With the reduced recoil I can use an extra $\frac{1}{8}$ ounce of shot, which will give me a better pattern at all ranges. The straight grip facilitates faster handling on those chances where one has only a momentary blur for a target.

Despite the storekeeper's advice, I shall continue to use No. 8 shot. It breaks more bones than the larger sizes, and breaking bones is the surest way to bring a grouse to earth. To those who scoff at using anything smaller than goose shot for upland hunting, I would like to point out that in the old days my partner and I hunted woodcock almost exclusively for the first two weeks of open season and used only No. 9 shot. We killed grouse with them, too, and many a black duck that we jumped from pools along the little brooks we followed. At twenty-five yards or less no grouse can fly through the center of an evenly distributed pattern of No. 9 and come out alive. I've proved that time after time, and I'm not Sam Smithers, no matter what my friends may say.

CHAPTER 20

40 Horsepower Dog[*]

Even before I lifted the phone I knew that it was H. G. Tapply calling, for that persuasive voice of his makes even the most blasé operator fluff her hair and put a bit of extra zing into her ring. "Look," Tap said, cutting quickly through the amenities, "are those grouse we found up in the Winnipesaukee country still there or have you annihilated them?"

"Do you think I'd run a blazer on an Associate Editor of *Field and Stream?*" I asked. "Those birds are joint property. I'm betting they're still there waiting for you to come up and help harvest them."

"'Good!" he said. "Now listen. Did you read that humorous thing of Ed Zern's that appeared in *Field and Stream* some time ago? The one about the mechanical bird dog he had invented— the Mechani-Mutt?"

"Yes," I said. "It was very funny. If I had his imagination I'd be writing best sellers."

"You ain't kiddin'," Tap said. "Do you know what he's dreamed up now?"

"Probably invented a flock of mechanical grouse for it to point," I suggested.

"No," he said seriously. Zern wrote that piece as a joke but it set him to thinking, and the more he thought about it the more he became convinced that the idea was practical. So he got a bunch of sports-minded scientists together and they built an electronic pointer—a transistor and battery-powered pooch. It has an air intake or nose that can distinguish between several

[*] Drink a lot of Bourbon before you read this chapter. Editor.

217

odors. It's still in the experimental stage, but they've put together a model that will work on grouse and woodcock. It's
guided by remote control, but when it picks up the proper scent
it homes in on it and traces it to its source. When the scent becomes strong enough it automatically stops and points. It's as
simple as that."

"Well, I'm simple, too," I reminded him, "but not simple
enough to swallow that."

"Don't kid yourself," he counseled. "I've got the thing out in
my back yard and it works. Zern wants us to try it in the field
and see if there are any mechanical kinks that need ironing out.
Will you be free tomorrow?"

"Probably not for long if they learn about this up at the booby
hatch," I said. "But until they strap me into a strait jacket I'm
at your command."

"Fine," he said. "Look for me around nine."

As a lover of bird dogs I must say that my first view of the
mechanical marvel was not an encouraging one. Although beautifully fabricated, it stood lifeless and cold in the station wagon's
luggage compartment. No pattering of eager feet, no friendly
tail wagging, no affectionate slavering. Its eyes were dull and
lusterless, and its whole attitude was that of a cast-iron lawn or-
nament.

But when Tap flipped the energy switch a startling transformation took place. The eyes suddenly glowed, hidden gears
whined, and a steady jet of air hissed audibly as it was sucked
into the single nostril. Somehow it sounded businesslike, and I
began to think that this riveted Roger might perhaps do some
remarkable things after all.

The thought was confirmed when Tap stopped at a tobacco
store for cigarettes. He had just disappeared within when a radi-
ant vision of femininity went tripping past. The morning was
warm, the car windows were down, and mingled with the soft

south wind that drifted through them I caught the unmistakable odor of Chanel No. 5.

I'm not blaming Ed Zern for what happened then—at least not much: after all, every inventor unconsciously incorporates some of his own personality into his brain child. As the entrancing odor permeated the air around us I heard the metallic Lothario give one long, ecstatic sniff and then let go with a real he-man wolf whistle.

Believe me, right there is one kink that needs ironing out. Up here in rock-ribbed New Hampshire a wolf whistle like that can land a fellow in the hoosegow. Tapply gave me a very peculiar look when he got back into the car.

Without further incident we got the power-packed pup to an isolated cover in the shadow of old Mount Belknap and proceeded to arm for action. For just a moment I felt a twinge of nostalgia for the old days when a brace of pointers would dance around us as they waited for the signal to hie on. Still, progress cannot be denied: so we shucked out the bells, whistles, choke collars and check-cords with which our pockets were stuffed, and filled them again with screwdrivers, pliers, socket wrenches, and other tools designed to cope with any malfunction that might occur. Then, while I set up the guns, Tap strapped on the radio-directional unit, flipped the power switch, and we were off.

I must confess that I was highly skeptical of the welded wonder's ability to negotiate our New Hampshire grouse covers. It might easily work the open fields and marshes, but the matted tangles in which our grouse are customarily found would give pause to a Sherman tank.

I was agreeably surprised, however. Its radar guided it unerringly around trees and huge boulders, yet let it scramble easily and effortlessly over all minor obstructions. It handled like a dream, too. With the delicately adjusted remote control, Tap could send it out on a long cast or bring it in to quarter faultlessly before us at a pace exactly suited to our needs.

The Mechani-Mutt.

A century or more ago this area had been farmland, hewed from the wilderness by hardy pioneers, but it had long since returned to the primitive. But it is excellent grouse country—a mecca for sportsmen in the good years and a sure bet for at least a few birds in the poorer ones.

We had moved perhaps two hundred yards when the mechanical marvel wheeled abruptly and went angling off to the left with an eagerness that was unmistakable, and we instinctively knew that the intricate membrane of the artificial nose had picked up warm grouse scent and was following it to its source. Deviating from its course only enough to slide past an occasional hindering tree, the power packed pooch followed the thread of scent unerringly. Then, at the base of a small, rounded knoll, it came to an abrupt stop, went ahead with infinite caution for another yard or two, halted once more, and slowly lifted a metallic front leg.

With awe and wonder we eased our guns forward and went in. As we drew near, Tap paused and whispered, "You take her. I'm not too sure about operating this contraption, but you kill the bird and I'll see what I can do about making this thing retrieve."

It has been my experience that a good grouse dog will not risk getting much closer than, say, five yards of a naturally jittery ruffed grouse. So I was startled when the bird burst out with a tremendous clatter from almost beneath that uplifted iron foot. Clumsily I slapped the gun to my shoulder and, with the muzzle a scant two feet from the delicate controls, pulled the trigger.

I missed the bird by a country mile, but that's a fact of little consequence in view of what happened next. With a whine of whirling gears and a frightened snort, Mr. Zerne's mechanical wonder went away from there like a turpentined tomcat. The astonished Tap, forgetting the controls that he held, hotfooted after it, loudly roaring "Whoa!"

The great experiment might have ended right there but for

the fact that the Mechani-Mutt misjudged the distance between two trees and jammed to a shuddering halt.

"Now I've seen everything," Tap said in awe. "Imagine—a cast-iron pooch that is gunshy."

The fault, we soon discovered, had been mine. The blast from my shotgun, discharged so near the sensitive controls, had jammed the setting to full-speed-ahead-and-damn-the-torpedos. The adjustment back to normal was quickly made and we were off once more.

It has been my good fortune to hunt over a few superlative grouse dogs, and by "superlative" I mean they had the ability to trail a running grouse both quickly and surely by body scent alone. It is a test that separates the potterers from the pros, and is the standard by which grouse dogs are judged. But good as they were, I must confess that I have never seen bird work like that we witnessed a few minutes later.

We had left the knoll and were working down a broad run of alders and scattered birches when the clanking canine slowed abruptly, then went stealthily ahead, all at once cat-footedly quiet, and weaving slightly from side to side as it centered the delicate thread of scent. I tingled to my toes, and Tap—hardened old grouse executioner that he is—grinned happily as he drew his side-by-side 20-gauge from under his arm.

On we went, down through the shallow run, across a brook, then up a gentle slope, while ahead went the automaton, pausing momentarily as the bird halted, then moving forward again unhurriedly but with a sureness that was heart warming. At the crest of the rise the trees thinned abruptly, and we could see an open glade fifty yards ahead. "It will lie when it reaches the opening," I whispered to Tap. "It's your meat."

"It is if it tries to cross that opening," he agreed, and hitched up his sleeves as we closed in on the metallic marvel that had now come to a quivering halt.

Somewhere near the edge of the opening the grouse, as I had

predicted it would do, had paused to consider the problem that now confronted it. Should it fly across the opening and risk the stoop of a sharp-eyed hawk, or cut back over our heads to the safety of the heavier growth? It was the latter course it chose, and rocketed up gloriously over the scanty trees. Tap centered it fairly and it spun limply down.

There is no more pleasing sight than that of a good dog coming joyously back with a lordly old cock grouse in its mouth, but I'm forced to admit that the Mechani-Mutt is a retrieving marvel. As Tap manipulated the controls it spun sharply around, maneuvered downwind until it caught the scent, then turned and went directly to the kill. Gentle mouthed, it brought the bird in without ruffling a feather.

It was then that the full significance of the invention dawned upon me. From mechanical dogs to mechanical birds is only a simple step. Once more our covers could resound to the thunder of a dozen birds rising simultaneously. Coveys of fifty quail could sit stoically as they waited for the electrical impulse that would send them whirring away. Armadas of mallards could circle in vast merry-go-rounds before hunters who wore asbestos gloves in deference to red-hot gun barrels. Gaudy cock pheasants, weighing 10 pounds each could populate every cornfield, while—

"Here, you manipulate this thing for a change," Tap said. "If it doesn't give you an uncanny feeling I miss my guess."

He was right. Handling that metal replica of a bird dog was an eerie piece of business. No need for whistling or shouting. No inflamed larynx. No breathless chasing after an elusive check cord. Just a slight touch of my finger on the sensitive controls made the Mechani-Mutt quarter faultlessly, increase its speed, slow down or come to a full stop.

Without the slightest difficulty I eased it up the hillside and headed it toward the car. We had almost reached the road when it stopped so suddenly that I knew it had come unexpectedly upon a closely crouched bird. For a moment it held steady, and then I saw it begin to weave slowly from side to side. With each passing second the movement increased until it was shimmying like a hula dancer in a cold wind.

For a moment I was puzzled, but then the answer dawned on me. The Mechani-Mutt was trying, with all its 40-horsepower, to simultaneously point two birds which were lying some distance apart. Fumbling with the controls, I clumsily switched the dial to full power, and for one wild moment I thought the thing would disintegrate like the deacon's one-hoss shay. But then I managed to reverse the switch and watched it calm down to a mere nervous twitching.

Tap, sensing the situation instantly, went hurrying ahead, and as the pair of birds went hurtling out he grassed them both with a snappy double. "That settles it in my mind," he said a few minutes later after the birds had been gathered in. "Old Ironsides is a whiz on grouse, but how will he do on woodcock? Let's go down to Tripwire and sick him on the timberdoodles."

The Tripwire cover was once a part of an extensive dairy-farm pasture that was rapidly returning to the wild. Dozens of barbed-wire entanglements still remained, half hidden among the ferns and bushes, and constituted a hazard to bones as old and brittle as mine. But every inch of it was woodcock country.

With Tap at the controls once more we set the Mechani-Mutt down at the edge of the cover, and it did not go twenty feet before it was on point. A flock of migrating birds had dropped in since we had last visited the place, and they were everywhere. So was our iron canine—finding dead birds, marking down misses, retrieving delicately. Its work, except for a slight tendency to shimmy when it located two or more birds at the same time, was faultless.

Only one thing marred the excellency of its performance. Although the prefabricated pup could slither around trees and climb over fallen logs as nimbly as a cat, those treacherous strands of barbed wire had it baffled for a time. Then at the next entanglement, before we could work in to unscramble it, the precocious pup reached down with its stainless steel jaws and snipped the wires as neatly as a telephone lineman could have done.

There's another kink that needs ironing out, believe me. Can you imagine what would happen in a dairy country if a dog started cutting every fence it came to? I made a mental note to tell Ed Zern to fit the next model with rubber dentures.

Scoring point after point, we worked down through the cover and came at last to a lush meadow where a half dozen Herefords were grazing inside an electric fence. The white insulators and shiny wire were new enough to indicate that the tightly stretched strand was potential dynamite, but the mechanical marvel paid it no heed. Emboldened perhaps by its previous success, it advanced on the lethal wire and clamped its metal jaws firmly upon it.

That was the only time I've seen a display of fireworks in broad daylight. Emitting brilliant flashes, and trailing sparks like a giant pinwheel, the Mechani-Mutt went round and round the wire like a trapeze performer around a horizontal bar, and would have been spinning there yet, I believe, had not centrifugal force come to its desperate need. With a last bluish burst of sparks the metal jaws slipped from their hold, and the tortured pup hit the ground with a resounding crash.

I may of course be wrong, but it is my opinion that the events which next occurred cannot be laid to faulty construction of the machine. It is far more likely that the prolonged electrical shock greatly increased the output of the batteries with which it was powered. If I am correct it would account for the tremendous energy which the thing now displayed.

No sooner had it struck the ground than it went into a series of violent convulsions not unlike those of a decapitated chicken. Leaping and somersaulting, and entirely unresponsive to Tap's frantic dialing, it went round and round in mad convolutions that made any attempt to stop it a hazardous undertaking indeed. But something had to be done if we were to keep it from destroying itself, so we circled it cautiously, like two strong-arm attendants in a violent ward, then plunged in and pinned it to earth while we closed the energy switch.

Reviewing the incident now, I can see that it would have been better if we had picked the machine up bodily and transported it to the car, but it presented a challenge to our ability, so we dug out our screwdrivers and pliers and fell to work, and after a dozen adjustments and as many startings and stoppings we managed to bring it under a measure of control.

I recall now that, as we started off once more, I was aware of a vague foreboding that all was not well with our prodigy. It moved jerkily, suddenly darting off at an oblique angle, or slowing down abruptly from no apparent cause. I spoke of it to Tap and he agreed with me.

"Something's gone wrong with its innards," he said. "It needs a factory overhaul. Let's work it up over that hill we skipped on the way down, get a few more points and then call it a day."

That is where we made our mistake. At the base of the hill we encountered a maze of blackberry vines that was almost impenetrable, and when we at last forced our way through it the panicky pup had disappeared, and it did not respond to the "Come in" signal that Tap was dialing.

Fanning out hastily, we searched for its trail, but precious minutes elapsed before we found it. My worst fears were verified. Entirely out of control, the Mechani-Mutt had gone up the hill in 10-foot leaps and was nowhere in sight. Panting from our efforts, we hurried along in its wake, and almost immediately were assailed by an odor that was unmistakable.

"A polecat!" Tap said. "The jeesly mutt has tangled with a wood pussy. What will we do now?"

"Is there a dial on that control that does something about skunks?" I asked.

"No," Tap said regretfully. "I guess that's another thing that Zern overlooked."

"Well," I said, holding my nose with a thumb and forefinger, "I guess that leaves it up to us."

So we started forward, and with each step we took the stench grew worse, until our eyes streamed water and we gasped for breath. Then, a hundred yards short of the crest of the hill, we came to the battle ground—a jumbled mass of fallen leaves, trampled ferns and freshly gouged earth. But no combatants— nothing but a freshly heaped mound of earth at the mouth of an old fox burrow. Then, as we stood there, we heard the sound of furious digging somewhere beneath our feet. At once every- thing became clear. The fast ranging automaton had blundered upon the skunk just outside the old burrow it was appropriating for its winter home. As a welcome it got both barrels at point blank range.

I could guess what happened. The overpowering scent had thrown the delicate nose of the apparatus into high gear. Every- thing in the machine was now concentrated on following that smell. The skunk had won the shelter of the burrow but its bloodthirsty adversary would not be denied its revenge. Some- where down there beneath our feet it was digging with might and main. Listening at the mouth of the burrow we could catch the muffled sound of gasping and gurgling and feral whining as the maddened mutt bored its way into the bowels of the earth.

Well, that's the story. We waited until long after darkness had fallen and the last faint sounds had ceased. It seems prob- able that down there somewhere in the twistings and turnings of the tunnel the crazed Mechani-Mutt had bypassed its quarry and continued digging straight on. Those powerful transistors will last practically forever, so it is certain that the creature will emerge again, but it will be in a field in China, and it will scare ten million peasants off the collective farms. Then an international crisis will arise. I'm glad that it is Ed Zern's name instead of mine that's on the mutt's collar.

CHAPTER 21

So Long, Pal

When I first met you the shooting season had ended, and the leaden New England skies seemed doubly cheerless because I had just lost your predecessor. Into that somber period of my life you came like a sun-kissed morning. I recall the day perfectly.

I was sitting morosely by the fire, pondering why a malicious fate so often casts a somber shadow over our lives. Then your owner drove into the yard with you and five of your brothers and sisters. I remember that when we opened the crates and you all came tumbling out pandemonium immediately ensued. Such leapings and twistings and turnings! Such mad dashings across the fields! Such a turmoil of yelpings which filled the air with their clamor, and dwarfed to nothing the exuberant cries of skaters rioting on the river, yet strangely it was a soothing sound to me. The leaden skies seemed to lighten, and all at once there was warmth and friendliness in the crisp December air.

I wish I might tell you that I knew from the first moment that you were going to be my dog, but that would not be strictly true. There were too many of your kind, a liver-and-white kaleidoscope that would not be still a moment. But gradually I became aware that there was one bit of atomic energy that frequently separated itself from its fellows and returned to its master for a friendly word. That was you, old boy. I knew you then. You were a one-man dog, and you were going to be mine.

I have never regretted my decision, and I like to think that in all the years we were together you never had occasion to regret it either. You see, I had formed an opinion concerning the ideal

229

relationship between a dog and its master which was somewhat at variance with my youthful conception of the status. I had learned that a dog was as much an individual as was a man, and I had come to believe that as long as it was compatible with good bird work, a dog should be encouraged to express his individuality. If he had his own ideas concerning the best way to handle a running pheasant or ruffed grouse, it might be better for me to modify my views slightly, instead of trying to mold the dog to my inflexible will.

I had vowed, too, that by every artifice at my command I would try to make my dog think that I was the most wonderful person in the world. He should be taught to mind promptly both signal and spoken commands, but there would be no hint of harshness in the teaching. Firmness, yes, but a gentle firmness that would leave no taint of unpleasantness for him to ponder over when he was alone.

And so I opened my home to you. You had your tufted pad in the kitchen. You owned one end of the davenport in the living room, and the upholstered chair in the den was yours by divine right. From the other rooms, and from the chambers, you were barred, but after you had worked your way into the heart of the gracious lady of the manor, I could sometimes hear the stealthy pad of your feet upon the stairs as you inched your way upward and into her room to wriggle an ecstatic good-morning welcome.

I remember how your soft brown eyes finally won for you, and how after a time you would remain there until you heard me open a door which led outside, when you would come tearing down, leaving a devastation of scattered rugs behind you, and vault in a long, arching curve out into your great and beautiful world.

Then you changed from a gangling six-months pup, whose feet and one end or the other were always a size too large, into a sleek and muscular creature whose every lithe movement was so graceful that it would cause a constriction in my throat just to watch you. We were compatible, you and I, for my system worked in your training. Five minutes time was all that was needed to teach you to hold as steady as a rock on your plate of food, and you won your sheepskin in retrieving after six easy lessons.

From the first day I took you afield you hunted with a joyous lightness that was my conception of perfection. Your nose spurned the earth as did your feet. You were airborne from the moment we entered a cover until we emerged from it, flitting here and there before me as smoothly as a swallow, while with your head uplifted you quested the air for game scent, yet slowing abruptly and advancing with tiptoeing caution whenever your unerring nose caught the first elusive fragment of it.

How wonderful they were, those first magic days that we spent together in the woods. The surrounding hills were no more immovable than you when you stretched out in one of your glorious points. No command of mine could move you as long as a ruffed grouse crouched in a thicket before you, as you proved to me on one of the very first days we hunted together.

You had disappeared from my sight in fairly thick cover, and after waiting a decent interval I drifted ahead with the hope that I would find you on point, but you were not there. With hurrying strides I went the length of the cover, and emerged into a more open one where only a few scattered pines grew. You were young and ambitious, and I thought the open country had challenged you to explore it; so I covered that, too, fearful lest I had lost you, and wondering if you had picked up enough woods lore to enable you to pick up my trail and follow it.

I was blowing my whistle then, shrilly and at frequent intervals and, still blowing it, I returned to that part of the cover where I had last seen you. There was one small opening in that tangle of birch and alders and by mere chance I blundered into one end of it. There you were at the other end, locked in a fiery point that a half hour of waiting had not quenched by a single degree.

There was always something about your points which made me a better man with a gun. You were so infallibly right when you slid into that animated but immobile pose, that it sometimes lifted me to supreme heights. So it was on that occasion. The grouse rose at a thirty yard range and had less than ten more to go to reach screening cover, yet I killed it without any sensation of hurrying and I had several feet to spare.

In the woods you were a dog who could be depended upon to the last minute of the last day, but at home you were sometimes unpredictable. I recall the occasion of Ray Holland's first visit with us. No one had told you that Ray was editor-in-chief of *Field and Stream,* and that he was paying for much of your bread and butter, or you might have acted differently.

Everything was normal for a time, and then that awkward moment arrived when conversation suddenly lagged. I was groping desperately for a topic, like a circus elephant wondering where the next peanut is coming from, when I thought of you.

You had a queer little trick of curling your right forefoot inward and lowering your head a trifle, and I had elaborated upon it until at a secret signal from me you would make a deep and exquisitely polite bow. We had rehearsed it until we had it perfected, and now it seemed like a life-saver. I went out and got you, put you smartly at heel, and we came in snappily like the well trained pair we were.

In the doorway I paused abruptly, said, "Pal, this is Ray Holland," and took one step aside, which was the cue to do your stuff. In that sudden and awful silence, you looked him calmly up and down, from his slightly thinning hair to the tips of his well-polished shoes—and yawned prodigiously. Then, with an air of melancholy that only Hamlet could have equalled, you turned and went back to the obscurity from which I had sum-

moned you, and curled up on your mat to resume your interrupted slumber.

There was another occasion when we entertained equally distinguished guests at dinner. Everything was painfully formal
and polite, and so far as real genial warmth was concerned we
might as well have been dining in an igloo. Then my ears detected a sound which filled me with startled apprehension. It
was the sound of your teeth clamping down on the metal rim of
your food pan. You came bounding in, your nails screeched as
they brought you to a skidding halt beside the table, you banged
the dish down on the floor, took a backward step and looked
expectantly up at us as though to say, "Hey, you guys! Don't I
rate a plate of food from a setup like this?"

You got the food, as you undoubtedly knew you would, and
it was the Most Distinguished Guest who passed the collection
plate, but even before you had finished bolting the last fragment
a miracle had taken place. All our stiff formality had vanished,
and we were really enjoying a friendship which has been a last-
ing one.

I remember, too, the day when you gave me the coldest bath
I have ever experienced. We were hunting woodcock in the
Nighthawk Cover, a mile-long strip of alder tangle through
which ran a brawling, turbulent brook. It was late in the season.
The ground had frozen the previous night, and even now with
the sun two hours high there was a rim of ice around the edges
of each upthrust boulder in the brook.

We had hunted the length of the cover, and now I was searching for a place where I could cross the stream. Ordinarily there
were numerous spots where one could step from stone to stone
and win the opposite bank with feet still dry; but on this day
the water was far above its normal level and the stepping-stones
were few and mighty far between.

I found a place which showed possibilities. It was not entirely
to my liking, for it required five jumps, and the third one—in

the center of the stream—was at least three feet out of line. The trick would have to be accomplished at high speed if it were accomplished at all, and I had a growing conviction that to pivot on that rounded boulder in midstream, and then spring off at a tangent for the remaining two, would require perfect co-ordination of both mind and muscle.

Standing on the bank, and deliberating the problem of which foot should touch which stone, I became so engrossed that I forgot another and equally important factor. The most rigid schooling I had given you consisted of crossing a street in the midst of heavy traffic. I would put you at heel and wait for a favorable opportunity. When it presented itself, I would tug mightily on your leash and we would shoot across the street in nothing flat. You learned to do it perfectly after a time, adjusting your pace to mine so accurately that we were never separated by more than a few inches. That was the factor I should have remembered.

Clutching the gun in one hand and my hat in the other, I leaped for the first boulder, and from the tail of my eye I saw your agile form take flight at the same moment. The situation, I could readily see, was about to become complicated unless I was man enough to beat you to the other shore. No boulder had room for more than one foot at a time, and to attempt to place five on it simultaneously could only result in disaster.

I beat you to the first one by inches, but we struck the second one together. Somehow I managed to secure enough leverage to make that twisting, third leap, and I made it with a sure foreknowledge of what was about to happen. It was necessary for me to achieve quite a bit of altitude in order to span the distance, but your wiry muscles gave you a flatter trajectory. You were fairly on the boulder and contracting your sinews for another leap when I came down upon you. You emitted one startled yelp, which was dwarfed to insignificance by my resounding splash, and then the icy waters closed over us.

You were the first ashore, and with a vigorous shake you were ready to go again, but I had to strip off the last dripping thread and wring the water from it. Ah, me! We were thirty miles from home, and we were hunting woodcock. We took our limit that day, with a brace of grouse thrown in for good measure, and we went home after night had fallen, dry and warm and inordinately happy.

One of the most satisfying things about the years we hunted together was the fact that I never knew you to fail to find a crippled bird. I believe a dog requires a far keener nose to locate dead or crippled game than he does to find an uninjured one, but whether or not this is true you had the thing required. You surprised me many times by bringing in a bird I believed I had missed cleanly.

There was a day when we were hunting woodcock along the shores of Lake Winnipesaukee. It was exceptionally open cover, and there was absolutely no excuse for missing any bird that got up within range; but I did it on a perfect straightaway. It was so entirely unexpected that I was disconcerted for a moment, and instead of redeeming myself with the second barrel I watched the bird fly a hundred yards and then flutter down into another sparse clump of alders.

You always gave me a puzzled look whenever I missed a bird, and on that occasion I could plainly read the question in your eyes. "What's the matter, boss?" they asked. "Slipping?"

I admitted it and told you to go find that woodcock. "Show him to me once more and I'll prove to you whether I'm slipping or not," I said, and you went down the cover and locked up on another of your spectacular points.

I kicked the bird out, killed it cleanly and sent you in to get it. Somehow you were never really enthusiastic about bringing in a woodcock. Knock down a grouse for you, and you would rush in and grab it, then come bounding back with a million dollar light in your eyes, but the little russet fellow always left you emotionally cold. Your attitude seemed to say, "It's swell sport hunting them, boss. I like to point them and I like to see you bowl them over, but what the heck do you care for them after they're dead?"

So you went dutifully in after the bird and started out with it. Then you hesitated, slowed to a walk, stopped, dropped the bird and began working the cover at your right.

I said to you, "Haven't you heard that a bird in the hand is worth two in the bush? Cut the fooling around, get down to business and bring me that bird."

You might have been deaf for all the attention you gave me. Methodically you quartered the thicket, swung sharply left, picked up a woodcock and came plodding out with it.

"I killed that first bird after all," I thought, but carefully refrained from voicing more than a polite thank you when you dropped it in my hand, for I was curious to learn if your reasoning powers were equal to the occasion.

If there was even a suspicion of doubt in my mind, I'm sorry for it, for of your own accord you went back and found the bird you had dropped, then came bounding back, passed it up to me, and your look seemed to say, "How's that, huh? Don't you think I'm a pretty good sort of guy to have around?"

I always thought you were. I miss you. Only yesterday I found myself pausing with my hand on the open door as I waited for the familiar thud of your feet as you landed beside me. You had an habitual disregard for those first three steps, and always went from the bottom to the top in one effortless leap. Undoubtedly I shall wait thus for you many more times. I wish it were possible for you to know that.

You left an impressive volume of memories for me to cherish, but of them all I think the last time we hunted together will remain clear the longest. For weeks I had known the disquieting feeling that you would not be with me much longer, but when the veterinarian told me so it came as a distinct shock. There had always been the hope that a miracle might happen, but now I could no longer hope. Yours was a tremendous vitality, for you rallied at times until you seemed almost your old self, but always when the relapse came you sank a little deeper into the abyss that awaited you.

Then the shooting season opened. I am very positive that you were aware of it, for your knowledge of many, many things was always a source of wonder to me. Your eyes followed my movements more closely during the hunting season, and once again I was keenly aware of them, even when you were apparently dozing before the fire.

Then one morning, after the frost had rimmed the lowlands with its white lace, you came to me with one of my hunting shoes in your mouth, and when I took it from you you went out and found its mate. "Want to go, do you?" I asked, and with all the animation your spent body could summon you answered "Yes."

I am glad that I decided as I did. My life has been richer because of those few last hours we spent together in the woods. There was a cover by the river, a scant three miles from home, that always held a few woodcock. By jouncing the car for a mile over corduroy roads I could put you within a half mile of it, and I knew your gallant heart could carry you the rest of the way. This day was yours. Nothing could take it from you.

You got down from the car like an old, old dog, but there was a crispness in the fall air, a heady odor to the moldering leaves which seemed to breathe new life into your emaciated frame. Your head came up, your questing nostrils searched the stirring air, and your lance-like tail assumed its old-time merriness.

You found a woodcock at the very edge of the cover, a second and third in a little depression near its center, and the fourth and last as we circled back to the outer edge. The legal limit was four, and we gathered them in with only four shells. Better than we had done on some other occasions you could recall, eh,

old pal? But it was fitting that it should end thus, for they were
the last woodcock your glorious nose would ever locate. When
you came out with that last bird your hunting days were over.
Finished. Done.

And you were done, too, old man. The fire which the day had
kindled in you flickered and died as we started back, and your
legs gave way beneath you. I gathered you up in my arms, an
almost lifeless load, and started back toward the car.

We had almost reached it when all at once I felt you stiffen
in my arms. For a moment a quick dread seized me, and then I
knew. Your head was uplifted. Your heavy eyes had opened wide
and assumed a new brightness. Your extended nostrils were expanded and drank in the crisp air in quick, excited inhalations.
Ruffed grouse! Somewhere in the thicket just ahead that mottled
brown king of the uplands crouched, poised on taut sinews for
its hurtling ascent. Ruffed grouse! Generations of your ancestors
had lived and died in order that there might be inculcated in
you an inherited instinct which made the scent of ruffed grouse
the acme of all your physical senses. It was the excuse for your
being. Without it you never could have lived.

I lowered you gently to your feet, a spent creature who had
shot his bolt and who was well-nigh done to death by an hour's
toil. You swayed in your weakness, but the magic of hot grouse
scent was in your nostrils and it was still potent. The trembling
left your legs, your head lifted and you took four cautious steps
ahead. A pause, another infinitely cautious step and you had it,
straight and true from the fountain head. You froze into immobility. A pitiful caricature of the thing of fire and bronze you
once were, but invincible still. You had nailed your grouse.

I pushed the gun forward and stepped up behind you, and in
that moment we became omnipotent. We were gods who ruled
that little kingdom of birch and alder and scented fir. You in
your infallibility had located the quarry, and I was possessed
with the sure knowledge that no tumultuous ascent, no artifice

of twisting or dodging which was his heritage could suffice it in this moment of its dire need. This thing had been foreordained. It was something which had to be.

The grouse came out on thundering wings, scattering the brown leaves beneath it with the wind from its takeoff. Upward it careened, a flashing, brown projectile, and your eyes watched the startled flight.

Then nitro crashed, and the bird hung limply in the air for a moment, suspended by its own inertia, before it hurtled down to set up a spasmodic drumming with its spent wings upon the fallen leaves.

"Dead bird," I said, and you went in and brought it out to me, and I could see a bit of heaven shining in your eyes.

I like, too, to remember the few last minutes we were together. You lay on your bed, covered by your blanket. The lethal dose of sleeping potion was already beginning to circulate in your veins. Your eyes were heavy, but in them there was contentment and peace.

Then a little pointer pup, a liver-and-white replica of what you must have been before I saw you, came up and sniffed a friendly greeting to you. Your eyes opened a trifle wider, and beneath your blanket your hard tail beat a friendly response. You extended your nose, sniffed your approval of the little stranger and bade him welcome. You knew there must always be other dogs, and so your great heart accepted him and shared him with the one you loved. It was all that was left for you to give. Then you yawned sleepily and closed your tired eyes.

So long, Pal.